# WATERLOO
## 1815

## GREGORY FREMONT-BARNES

## DUNDURN
### TORONTO

This book is dedicated to the memory of my mother, who gave unswervingly of her time, energy and love to her children.

All images supplied from the author's collection.

First published by Spellmount, an imprint of The History Press, 2012

Copyright © The History Press, 2012, 2015, 2016

Gregory Fremont-Barnes has asserted his moral right to be identified as the author of this work.

Printed in India

North American edition published by Dundurn Press, 2016

ISBN 978 1 4597 3402 9
A Cataloguing-in-Publication record for this book is available from Library and Archives Canada.

This book is also available in electronic formats: ISBN 978 1 4597 3403 6 (pdf); ISBN 978 1 4597 3404 3 (e-pub).

Visit us at
Dundurn.com | @dundurnpress | Facebook.com/dundurnpress
Pinterest/dundurnpress

Dundurn
3 Church Street, Suite 500
Toronto, Ontario, Canada
M5E 1M2

# CONTENTS

# INTRODUCTION

Waterloo holds an enduring, international appeal, with greater attention than ever focusing on the event as the bicentenary approaches in 2015. Accounting for this fascination amongst scholars, students, lay readers, historical re-enactors and wargamers poses little challenge, for few battles combine so many separate, but each compelling, struggles within a greater contest of arms: the stubborn defence of Hougoumont; the fight for the little farm of La Haie Sainte; the charge of the French heavy cavalry against Wellington's centre; the bitter street-fighting in Plancenoit; the attack of Napoleon's Imperial Guard; and a host of other remarkable episodes whose outcome in nearly every case remained in the balance until evening.

Waterloo offers a glimpse into the events of a single day whose salient features appear to bear little resemblance to the experience of combat familiar to us today. The 'invisible battlefield' – that eerie environment shaped by the lethality of fire which so often separates combatants to the extent that they become effectively unseen – has brought a cold, impersonal detachment to what the soldiers of 1815 understood as a very intimate business of killing. The pathos associated with men deployed shoulder to shoulder, following a strict evolution of drill in order to load and fire their muskets in volleys at their geometrically arranged opposites

*Napoleon in 1815. He could not hope to consolidate his newly restored power without defeating the two Allied armies in the Low Countries before the far larger Austrian and Russian armies reached France from the east. The best prospect for victory therefore rested with a strategy designed to defeat the Allies in detail, a course which obliged Napoleon to assume the offensive immediately, make a dash into Belgium and confront the Anglo-Allied and Prussian armies in separate, hopefully decisive, engagements thereby preventing the two armies from uniting and overwhelming the emperor through sheer weight of numbers.*

from harrowingly short distances; and the dramatic spectacle of horsemen, resplendent in impractical but superbly colourful uniforms, wielding sword or lance, holds a particularly romantic appeal to those who, with considerable justice, believe that war since 1914 has reduced mankind to new depths of inhumanity – even barbarism – sullied by the substitution of machines for men, by the horrors associated with the mass destruction of civilians from 20,000ft and by conflicts waged for less honourable motives than those of an apparently lost, halcyon age.

# Introduction

The act of men standing opposite one another, blazing away like rival firing squads until the steadiness of one side or the other breaks under the pressure of fire or the impact of a bayonet assault somehow sparks the imagination, reminding us of the extraordinary courage required of soldiers who could, quite literally, see the whites of the enemy's eyes. Waterloo marked the beginning of the end of chivalry, with 1914 signalling its final demise, as Andrew Roberts observed:

> Ghastly as the carnage at Waterloo undoubtedly was, thenceforth wars were to be fought with the infinitely more ghastly methods of trenches (the Crimea), barbed wire, railways and machine-guns (the American Civil War), directed starvation (the Franco-Prussian War), concentration camps (the Boer War), and mustard gas and aerial bombardment (the First World War). By the time of the Great War, chivalry was effectively dead as an element of war-making.
>
> Roberts, *Waterloo*, p.15

Eyewitness accounts of extraordinary devotion to duty abound – adding further to the appeal of this subject. Sir Edward Creasy, the Victorian author of *The Fifteen Decisive Battles of the World*, related a number of examples of this spirit:

> Never, indeed, had the national bravery of the French people been more nobly shown. One soldier in the French ranks was seen, when his arm was shattered by a cannon-ball, to wrench it off with the other; and throwing it up in the air, he exclaimed to his comrades, 'Vive l'Empereur jusqu' à la mort!'... [A]t the beginning of the action, a French soldier who had both legs carried off by a cannon-ball, was borne past the front of Foy's division, and called out to them, 'Ce n'est rien, camarades; Vive l'Empereur! Glorie à la France.' The same officer, at the end of the battle, when all hope was lost, tells us that he saw a French grenadier, blackened with powder, with his clothes torn

9

and stained, leaning on his musket, and immovable as a statue.
The colonel called to him to join his comrades and retreat; but
the grenadier showed him his musket and his hands; and said
'These hands have with this musket used to-day more than
twenty packets of cartridges: it was more than my share: I
supplied myself with ammunition from the dead. Leave me to
die here on the field of battle. It is not courage that fails me,
but strength'.

Creasy, London, 1877, p.614

Little wonder Waterloo continues to grip the imagination.

On a grand strategic level, it signified the end of an era – of over
a century of conflict with France, with whom Britain would never
again cross swords. Indeed, the two nations would co-operate in
the Crimea forty years later and, of course, again in the two World
Wars. It also marked the end of any further French attempts at
territorial aggrandisement in Europe – which largely accounts for it
also signifying the end of the long period of Anglo-French hostility,
dating from the great conflict against Louis XIV which began
in 1689 – though some may trace it back to the Hundred Years
War if not to the Norman invasion. The comprehensive nature of
Waterloo led to Napoleon's final downfall and the re-drawing of
the map of Europe, with central Europe rationalised into a few
dozen, instead of a few hundred states – thereby setting the stage
for German unification later in the century. As Andrew Roberts
put it: '…it ended forever the greatest personal world-historical
epic since that of Julius Caesar…'. Waterloo not only ended a
generation of conflict, it put paid to such a blood-letting as Europe
had not experienced since the religious wars of the seventeenth
century and ushered in a hundred years of comparative peace.
True, there were wars yet to be fought – the Crimean and those of
Italian and German unification; but these paled into insignificance
as compared with the sheer scale of the conflicts unleashed on
Europe by the French revolutionaries in 1792, belatedly but
definitively crushed in Belgium twenty-three years later. It was not

for nothing that contemporary Britons referred to this period as 'The Great War' a century before the term was applied again in another, far more horrifying context.

Waterloo is not significant as representing a passing era of warfare and the beginning of a new phase, for the weaponry arrayed there bore a great deal in common with that deployed by the Duke of Marlborough's army over a century earlier, and warfare on land would not undergo any genuinely significant change until the 1850s, with the application of rifling to small arms and, later, artillery, followed rapidly by the advent of breech-loading technology. But if the subtle differences between the weapons employed on either side at Waterloo did not palpably contribute to its outcome, the tactics employed there certainly did. In the absence of any great flanking movements on the battlefield, Waterloo amounted to a great slogging match, with the balance between victory and defeat depending heavily upon the degree of French determination to press home the attack and the stubbornness with which the Anglo-Allies were prepared to receive that attack. The fact that both sides fought with remarkable energy and spirit contributes all the more to the appeal of a subject which remains a great epic in the history of the British Army. Not for nothing Waterloo continues to be one of history's greatest battles.

# TIMELINE

| | |
|---|---|
| **20 April 1792** | France declares war on Austria, thereby initiating the Revolutionary Wars |
| **1 February 1793** | France declares war on Britain and Holland. In the course of the coming months the Allies form the First Coalition |
| **5 April and 22 July 1795** | By the Treaties of Basle, Prussia and Spain leave the First Coalition |
| **17 October 1797** | France and Austria conclude the Treaty of Campo Formio, effectively ending all continental resistance to Revolutionary France and marking the end of the Second Coalition |
| **25 March 1802** | Britain concludes the Treaty of Amiens with France, ending the Revolutionary Wars |
| **18 May 1803** | After a brief hiatus, hostilities between Britain and France resume, so marking the beginning of the Napoleonic Wars |
| **11 April 1805** | Russia and Britain conclude an alliance, later joined by Austria (9 August) and Sweden (3 October), which results in the formation of the Third Coalition |

# Timeline

| | |
|---|---|
| **2 December 1805** | Napoleon decisively defeats combined Austro-Russian army at Austerlitz, thereby destroying the Third Coalition |
| **14 October 1806** | The French decisively defeat the Prussians in the twin battles of Jena and Auerstädt |
| **7–9 July 1807** | France, Prussia and Russia conclude the Treaties of Tilsit, effectively acknowledging Napoleon's extensive dominion west of the river Niemen on the Polish-Russian frontier |
| **14 July 1807** | The Battle of Friedland, fought in East Prussia, puts paid to the last vestiges of Prussian as well as, more importantly, Russian resistance to French control of most of the European mainland |
| **2 May 1808** | A popular uprising in Spain marks the beginning of open resistance throughout Iberia against French control |
| **1 August 1808** | Forces under Sir Arthur Wellesley (the future Duke of Wellington) land in Portugal, marking the beginning of British participation in the Peninsular War |
| **5–6 July 1809** | Battle of Wagram, the decisive battle of Napoleon's campaign against a resurgent Austria, which concludes peace on 14 October at Schönbrunn |
| **22 June 1812** | Napoleon leads the *Grande Armée* of over half a million men into Russia |
| **22 July 1812** | Wellington defeats the French at Salamanca in central Spain, thereby opening the way for a major Anglo-Portuguese offensive to clear Iberia |
| **19 October 1812** | Having failed to bring the Russians to terms, Napoleon abandons Moscow and begins to retreat west, with disastrous consequences |
| **21 June 1813** | At Vitoria, Wellington inflicts a decisive defeat on the main French army in Spain |

| | | |
|---|---|---|
| **1813** | 16–19 October | A colossal Allied force consisting of Austrians, Prussians, Russians and Swedes decisively defeats Napoleon's army at Leipzig, in Saxony, forcing it to abandon Germany and cross back into France |
| **1814** | 6 April | After failing to hold back the Allies in a remarkable but ultimately unsuccessful campaign on home soil, Napoleon abdicates |
| | 30 April | (First) Treaty of Paris concluded between France and the Allies |
| | 1 November | The Congress of Vienna convenes to re-draw the map of Europe after a generation of war led to the abolition of some states, the creation of others and the shifting of the frontiers of practically all the rest |
| **1815** | 26 February | Napoleon leaves exile on Elba for France |
| | 1 March | Napoleon lands on the south coast of France |
| | 19 March | Louis XVIII leaves Paris for the safety of Ghent in Belgium |
| | 20 March | Napoleon arrives in Paris and returns to power, marking the beginning of his 'Hundred Days' |
| | 25 March | The Allies declare Napoleon an outlaw and form the Seventh Coalition |
| | 16 June | Battles of Ligny and Quatre Bras |
| | 18 June | Battles of Waterloo and Wavre |
| | 22 June | Napoleon abdicates |
| | 20 November | (Second) Treaty of Paris concluded between France and the Allies |

# HISTORICAL BACKGROUND

In seeking to understand the Allies' motives for wishing to defeat Napoleon, one must examine, if only in brief, the wars spawned by the French Revolution in 1792 which, apart from a short period of peace between March 1802 and May 1803 , finally came to an end in the spring of 1814. The first phase of this fighting, known as the Revolutionary Wars, arose out of two principal requirements of the new republic: one ideological and the other strategic. In the case of the former, the French sought to spread the principles of the Revolution abroad, specifically by appealing to the populations of the Low Countries, Switzerland, the Rhineland and northern Italy to throw off, as the revolutionaries characterised it, the yoke of monarchical despotism which represented the tyranny, corruption and system of privilege which the French themselves had cast off in the first years of social and political turmoil following the fall of the Bastille in 1789. Having seized that great fortress and prison – the very symbol of monarchical oppression – the revolutionaries established a national assembly and eventually curbed the powers of the king, Louis XVI, later declaring a republic, adopting a series of constitutions and, finally, executing their monarch in January 1793 – as much to hail the triumphs of the Revolution as to offend the crowned heads of Europe, many of whom, by that time, had already seen the Revolution for what it was – a threat to their ideological well-being and the principle of legitimacy. Appreciating, too, that so much power as that gathered in the hands of men clearly dangerous to European security – quite apart from the obvious threat to monarchical rule – Austria, Prussia, Holland, Spain and numerous smaller states went to war with France as early as April 1792.

*The Battle of Jemappes, 6 November 1792, the second major French victory against the forces of the First Coalition, fought near Mons in the Austrian Netherlands (modern Belgium). After the decisive engagement at Fleurus in June 1794, France formally annexed the country the following year and thereafter conscripted extensively there for the next twenty years. This explains why, during the Waterloo campaign, many of Wellington's Belgian troops had served Napoleonic France. The story was much the same for the Dutch, the French having conquered Holland in 1795 and absorbed it into the empire in 1810.*

The combined strength of this, the First Coalition, ought to have crushed the Revolution in short order; but through bungled strategy, competing war aims, indecisiveness and military incompetence in the face of the new, energetic and, above all, massive conscripted armies of the French republic, the Allied powers repeatedly failed to bring the revolutionaries to heel, forming in fact two impressive coalitions in the decade between 1792 and 1802 without accomplishing more than enabling France to expand her borders to an extent never even dreamed of by Louis XIV: the whole of the Low Countries, the west bank of the Rhine, the Alps (thus including parts of northwest Italy) and the Pyrenees – the so-called natural frontiers. In fact, there was nothing 'natural' about them at all, apart from the southern frontier with Spain, which had remained more or less unchanged for centuries. The French, not content merely to defend their own soil against, admittedly, those bent on the destruction of what amounted to wholesale improvements in the political, social and economic lives of millions of French citizens, took possession by force of arms these vast swathes of new territory, justifying these extraordinary conquests on the cynical basis that annexation, occupation or the imposition of some form of dependent status on the conquered inevitably benefitted them all. Who, the argument ran, could fail to appreciate the advantages bestowed by the Revolution? Accordingly, where neighbouring lands escaped outright annexation, they found themselves controlled either directly or indirectly from Paris – not quite akin to the Eastern European experience of Soviet control in the wake of the Second World War – but something of a precursor to that phenomenon. Those states with the temerity to oppose the 'liberators' paid a heavy price: military intervention, forced requisitioning, the imposition of indemnities and, in many cases, outright annexation.

Disagreements within the Allied camp strongly contributed to the collapse of the First Coalition, a process begun as early as 1795, when Spain and Prussia, demoralised by failure to make progress against the growing strength of the republic, unilaterally

*The retreat from Moscow. The emperor leads the vanguard of the ever-dwindling Grande Armée out of Russia. Determined to rebuild his army for the coming campaign in the spring of 1813 and to forestall a coup in Paris, he absented himself at Smorgi and made his way by sledge to Poland and thence to France.*

abandoned their allies, which now included Britain since February 1793. After Austria suffered a series of humiliating defeats in her former Belgian possessions, along the Rhine and, above all, across northern Italy between 1796 and 1797, she concluded the Treaty of Campo Formio, which marked the death knell of the First Coalition. A resurgent Austria, still supported by Britain and joined by Russia, Turkey and others, formed the Second Coalition in 1798–99, with some initial success. The Allies recovered all of northern Italy from the French, Russian forces managed to penetrate as far west as Switzerland and even co-operated with the British in Holland in 1799, but they withdrew from the fighting, leaving Britain practically on her own in 1801, once Austria concluded a separate peace with France at Lunéville after suffering decisive twin defeats the previous year at Marengo and Hohenlinden. Thus, with an *impasse* created by French dominance

*Napoleon at the Battle of Marengo, 14 June 1800, the last of his long string of victories over the Austrians during the French Revolutionary Wars. This decisive blow, in combination with General Moreau's triumph at Hohenlinden six months later, obliged Austria to sue for peace despite her agreement with the other members of the Second Coalition not to withdraw from the alliance on a separate basis.*

on land and British supremacy at sea, the two hereditary enemies agreed to peace at Amiens in the spring of 1802. No one could deny that, in standing utterly triumphant on the Continent – with the consequent radical shift in the balance of power – France reaped the lion's share of the benefits accruing to those nations now wearied by a decade of conflict.

French claims that the republic required buffer states to protect her from her ideological rivals rang hollow during the interlude of peace inaugurated at Amiens. If Britain could grudgingly accept by 1802 that the principles of the Revolution – admirable though most of them were – had been thrust upon France's neighbours at the point of the bayonet and remained an incontestable fact of life in western Europe, she could not long tolerate the strategic imbalance which French occupation represented or the control of the belt of satellite states created to enhance and extend French power beyond historically accepted bounds. The renewal of war thus remained inevitable even before the ink had dried at Amiens. Accordingly, hostilities resumed in May 1803, first in the form of a strictly Anglo-French conflict, but by the summer of 1805 it was to expand into a full-fledged coalition – the Third. By this time the Allies had ceased to insist upon the restoration of the Bourbon monarchy and concentrated simply on deposing Napoleon and restraining the over-arching power of an expansive, now imperial, France. That nation no longer represented an ideological threat – the fact that Napoleon had reigned in constitutionalism and established himself as virtual dictator confirmed the fact. Yet, again, the Allies' endeavour to re-establish a degree of strategic equilibrium on the Continent failed – and in shorter order than ever before – thanks to the capitulation of an entire Austrian army

*General Mack surrendering his entire army of 30,000 Austrians in October 1805 at Ulm, a precursor of even more disastrous events to befall the Allies at Austerlitz, the most decisive victory in Napoleon's career, on 2 December. By the Treaty of Schönbrunn Austria abandoned the Third Coalition, leaving the Russians to retreat east into Poland to lick their wounds and await another opportunity to oppose the seemingly unbeatable forces of the Grande Armée.*

at Ulm in October 1805, followed six weeks later by Napoleon's decisive victory at Austerlitz, near Vienna, which led to the coalition's collapse. Napoleon, flushed with victory, renewed his self-seeking bid for further territorial gain, a process rendered all the more permanent when he placed various members of his family on the thrones of some of his dependencies.

By establishing the Confederation of the Rhine in July 1806, Napoleon could levy financial contributions as well as troops from a host of German states – some large like Bavaria and Saxony, some small like Hesse-Darmstadt and Mecklenburg. In his efforts to extend French influence well beyond central Europe, the emperor directly or indirectly controlled the whole of the Italian peninsula and the Dalmatian coast, such that when, upon crushing the resurgent Russians at Friedland in June 1807, and concluding accords with Russia and Prussia at Tilsit, Napoleon possessed a free hand with which to create a Polish satellite state known as the Duchy of Warsaw, thus providing him control over the whole of the Continent from the Atlantic in the west to Denmark and the Prussian coast in the north, to the toe of Italy and the Adriatic coast in the south and to the Russian frontier in the east. In three short years Napoleonic armies had cowed the three great continental powers of Austria, Russia and Prussia – a military feat not repeated until Germany's stunning successes in the early years of the Second World War. Britain, though supreme at sea, particularly after Trafalgar in October 1805, could accomplish little on land apart from seizing French colonies in the West Indies and dispatching largely ineffectual expeditionary forces to the Continent. To be fair, she could, and did, fund her allies generously with millions of pounds in subsidies; but in the wake of such catastrophes as Austerlitz, Jena and Friedland, financial aid proved woefully insufficient in reversing the hegemony imposed by France in the wake of the remarkable string of victories which marked out the Napoleonic heydays of 1805–07.

Three more coalitions followed, with the Sixth (1813–14) finally successful in April 1814 in subduing France, forcing Napoleon's abdication and exile to the tiny Mediterranean island of Elba and restoring the Bourbon dynasty in the person of Louis XVIII, with whom came a new charter designed not as a reactionary doctrine to return an exhausted and war-weary France to the *status quo ante bellum* – which even the monarchists understood to be both unrealistic and unworkable – but to provide for a parliamentary government which, at least in principle and appearance, would rival any found elsewhere in Europe. The king's rule was to be established on a limited basis, including consultation with ministers and assistance provided by a bicameral (two-chamber) legislature composed of a House of Peers nominated by Louis, as well as an assembly composed of electors eligible by virtue of their annual tax contribution.

Quite sensibly, the king agreed that the very sizeable tracts of land once the property of the Crown and Church which the revolutionaries had sold off in the course of the 1790s ought to remain in the hands of their new owners, many of whom by 1814 could therefore trace their new acquisitions back more than two decades. The new constitution guaranteed civil liberties, while many of the institutions and much of the bureaucracy of the imperial years the royalist government retained with little amendment. The Restoration amounted, in effect, to a compromise, with the upper middle class accepting, albeit with some disgruntled protest, a new order which limited the power of the franchise while according to them, via a conservative legislature, the responsibility for enacting laws and levying taxes. If the broad public no longer enjoyed the influence upon politics which had constituted their new right from the earliest days of the Revolution, that memory now appeared a distant one in any event, for Napoleon's seizure of power as First Consul in 1799 had largely put paid to the notion that the Revolution must continue to undergo a state of perpetual change.

Yet in less than a year this system began to break down, so creating the widespread atmosphere of discontent from which Napoleon could profit by plotting his return to power.

The government of Louis XVIII revealed itself much less sympathetic to liberal constitutionalism than the rhetoric of its first days in power implied, and in so doing alienated not merely individuals on a broad scale, but whole sectors of society wielding varying degrees of power, and whose voices and sentiments the new regime could only ignore at its peril. In practice, the Bourbons accepted no genuine admission of responsibility for rule based on cabinet government. Ministers advised and reported to the king on an individual basis and could – and regularly did – ignore the legislature, particularly the Chambers. Many former courtiers, returned from exile or at the very least from obscurity within France, gathered in the Tuileries in a manner alarmingly reminiscent of the days prior to the fall of the Bastille.

In the army, much of the Napoleonic officer corps was retired on half-pay and replaced with sycophants and many of the breed of aristocrats whom the revolutionaries had long ago and with entire justification removed from their posts on grounds ranging from simple incompetence to disloyalty to the new political realities of republicanism. To compound these problems, an increasing number of hopefuls – some perhaps deserving, most certainly not – lobbied for a restoration of their former privileged status, including *émigré* officers, priests and nobles. The ultra-royalists, in particular, sought a wholesale reversal of political affairs and made no attempt to conceal their contempt for a charter which they connived to replace with a restored, absolutist order. Personally, in his nonchalant attitude to the affairs of state and general neglect of business, Louis exhibited every sign of sympathy with the ultras, who therefore looked optimistically upon the prospect of achieving their objectives of reversing many features of political and social progress whose retention practically everyone else – that is, widely different spectra of French society – could agree upon.

Moreover, just as the royalists revelled in restoring the old order, so many former officers and civil servants, jettisoned from their positions upon the fall of the Empire in April 1814, longed for the return of Napoleonic rule. Many wished to re-establish the

23

*European foreign ministers and diplomatic representatives, including the Duke of Wellington* (standing, centre) *in his new capacity as ambassador to France, assembled at the Congress of Vienna. No precedent existed for an international gathering on this scale; but a generation of radical changes to the map of Europe now obliged all the major and many of the minor states to reconfigure borders based on a host of considerations, some of them contradictory: legitimacy, security and, for their pains, territorial compensation to the key Allied powers.*

nation's military prowess and thus extinguish the humiliation of defeat; others opposed the new regime on the ideological grounds that, notwithstanding the restrictions imposed on civil rights by the Napoleonic state, many of the gains achieved during the Revolution had remained largely or wholly untouched down to the fall of the Empire, only now to be tampered with by Bourbons; indeed, the introduction of the Napoleonic Code in 1802 had built upon these sweeping, often egalitarian reforms. This is not to claim that the nation as a whole enthusiastically longed for the emperor's return; the only truly reliable base of support was to be found amongst much, though by no means all, of the peasantry and former soldiers. No one sought a return to the blood-letting that had left hundreds of thousands of French soldiers dead since 1792; but nor did they wish to return to pre-revolutionary conditions for whose destruction the nation had paid so high a price over the course of a generation.

The Allied governments, whose diplomatic representatives had sat at Vienna since the peace in order to re-establish some semblance of territorial logic out of the Continent's radically re-drawn borders, immediately declared their determination to oppose Napoleon personally – for this, the Seventh Coalition, was not to constitute a war waged against France as such, but a struggle against an illegitimate regime. Cries of righteous indignation from Napoleon in Paris that he intended to pursue a policy of peace towards his neighbours; that internal reform would mark his reign; and that he desired no territorial gains – and thus renounced all claims to foreign soil – fell on deaf ears, or rather on those for whom the emperor's past record of conquest rendered his promises very hollow indeed. Perhaps Napoleon genuinely sought to live in harmony with his neighbours and that the dispatch of Allied armies towards the French frontier accounted for the emperor's immediate decision to mobilise his resources; yet whatever the truth of the matter, the historical record comprehensively failed to assuage the anxieties of those who branded Napoleon an international pariah bent on re-imposing French hegemony over the whole of Europe.

# THE ARMIES

## A Brief Overview

Immediately at Napoleon's disposal stood the 200,000 men of Louis' army, whose loyalty to the returned emperor carried over from the numerous previous campaigns in which many such troops had participated. Napoleon immediately set about supplementing this force by recalling men from leave, drafting in repatriated prisoners and discharged veterans, inducting sailors into the army and appealing for volunteers. Potential manpower stood high, but the rapidity of events denied him the use of the nearly 50,000 men furnished by the class of 1815, who did not reach the army in the field before Waterloo.

The emperor renamed his principal force *l'Armée du Nord*, which numbered 123,000 men and 350 guns at the outset of the campaign. Smaller contingents, but totalling 104,800 troops, were deployed on the other frontiers, for consolidating the whole disposable force – even if time enabled such an ambitious and vast enterprise – would have left the borders totally exposed. Besides, forces were also required to discourage unrest and suppress actual rebellion. In due course, Napoleon could confidently expect his field army to rise above 200,000 men. Apart from limited numbers, his army suffered from serious shortages of weapons, horses and equipment as a consequence of the previous regime's neglect. Napoleon began to remedy these deficiencies from the moment he returned to power, such that by the time *l'Armée du Nord* took the field, it possessed the requisite amount of matériel and represented a formidable, highly motivated fighting force.

The force commanded by the Duke of Wellington was of a very different complexion to that magnificent fighting machine he had commanded in the Peninsula and southern France between 1808 and 1814. Peace in 1814 had led to an immediate reduction of numbers in the British Army, while at the same time regiments were diverted directly from French ports for service against the United States, at war with Britain since June 1812. Some of the units which remained in Belgium had fought in Iberia, but others had taken part in the unsatisfactory operations in Holland the previous year and did not match the standard of Peninsular veterans.

*French troops skirmishing with British cavalry during the Anglo-Portuguese retreat to Busaco, in eastern Portugal, in 1810. Although the troops on both sides possessed years of experience fighting one another in the Peninsula, Napoleon and Wellington had never met in battle before Waterloo owing to the former's very short period of command in Spain. Instead, while he campaigned elsewhere, the emperor left the fighting in Iberia to his subordinates.*

## Typical French Soldier

A French infantryman, or fusilier, carried a knapsack supported by straps which extended over the shoulder and under the armpit, plus a leather cartridge box suspended on a belt slung over the left shoulder. Often he wore a second belt over the right shoulder which carried a bayonet or a short sword. He invariably carried a canteen, plus a rolled greatcoat or blanket either fastened on top of his knapsack or slung diagonally across his front or back. He usually also carried a mess tin and haversack. The burden of all this equipment, including several day's supply of rations, changes of clothes and various personal effects, could weigh as much as 60lb – quite apart from his musket. Soldiers probably valued their boots above all other items of clothing and equipment, for unless well-shod he was destined to the miserable experience of marching barefoot. During the Waterloo campaign he lived in a bivouac with nothing more to protect him than the shelter of his blanket or greatcoat.

A soldier passed his time in camp with letter-writing, gambling, playing music and telling stories. His lot generally consisted of marching, establishing camp, cleaning his weapon, and drill. Officers expected strict discipline and although they had largely long since ceased to strike their soldiers in the ranks to ensure the proper alignment of the ranks, flogging remained the principal corporal method of punishing serious infractions, such as sleeping on duty or, above all, desertion. Rations varied according to availability, but a typical infantryman could expect a sufficient quantity of bread, cheese, meat and wine on a daily basis, particularly during the Waterloo campaign, when the shortness of the operations caused no shortage of supplies. If not actually conscripted, a soldier might join the ranks for a number of motives, usually a combination of several: the desire for comradeship and a sense of belonging to the extended 'family' which the army represented; a chance for adventure and possibly even 'glory', however an individual chose to define that elusive but well-respected concept; promotion within an institution famous for its egalitarian culture; as an alternative to prison, if a magistrate offered such an option; but, above all, an escape from poverty, for the army provided regular food, pay and accommodation, even if on a rudimentary scale.

## Napoleon I, Emperor of the French (1769–1821)

Few military or political figures have stamped their impression so strongly on an epoch than Napoleon, who rose from fairly humble origins on Corsica to the throne of France at the age of thirty-five. After schooling in France in the 1780s, he established a name for himself during the siege of Toulon in 1793. He played an instrumental role in protecting his political masters two years later when with his guns he swept the streets clear of a Royalist mob, in recognition for which in 1796 the government appointed him commander-in-chief of the army in Italy. In the course of his campaign against the Austrians Napoleon demonstrated both strategic and tactical brilliance, securing an exceptionally favourable peace settlement for his country – not to mention an enhanced military reputation for himself. After an abortive campaign in Egypt and Palestine in 1798–99, the young general returned to France and instigated a *coup d'état*. After crossing the Alps in 1800 and drubbing the resurgent Austrians in a lightning campaign, he promulgated the Napoleonic Code and other social and political reforms before crowning himself emperor in 1804. His subsequent successes in the field – in which he decisively defeated the forces of Austria, Prussia and Russia in a series of brilliant campaigns between 1805 and 1807 – marked the high-water mark of his military career. Blind ambition, however, soon got the better of him, and his ill-fated adventures, first in Iberia from 1808 and then in Russia four years later, opened cracks in Napoleon's hitherto seemingly invulnerable empire, and in the campaigns fought successively in Germany and France in 1813–14, the beleaguered emperor found himself on the defensive, eventually overwhelmed by an irresistible coalition which captured Paris and forced the emperor's abdication – albeit temporarily – for he returned briefly to power during the 'Hundred Days', when comprehensive defeat at Waterloo put a definitive end to the era that aptly bears his name.

*The greatest commander since Alexander the Great, Napoleon led forces at more than sixty battles between 1796 and 1815, with some of his most impressive fought during the Allied invasion of France little more than a year before the Waterloo campaign.*

# Arthur Wellesley, 1st Duke of Wellington (1769–1852)

The most successful of the many commanders who fought the French over the course of a generation, he was the fourth son of the Earl of Mornington, a minor member of the Anglo-Irish aristocracy. Wellesley joined the army in 1787, fighting his first action in Flanders in 1794 before being sent to India four years later. Thanks to the position of his brother, Richard, as governor general, he commanded troops at the great siege of Seringapatam in 1799, demonstrating remarkable skills in staff work. Thereafter Wellesley fought in successive campaigns in southern India, most notably the campaign against the Mahrattas in 1803 when, massively outnumbered at Assaye, he defied the odds and routed his opponents. By the time he commanded the expeditionary force to Portugal in August 1808 Wellesley possessed a reputation for a high degree of efficiency, particularly on logistical matters. He immediately proved himself fit for so important a command, achieving success at Roliça and Vimeiro, where he began the long series of virtually unbroken Peninsular victories down to 1814 for which he is justly celebrated. Raised to the peerage as Marquis (and eventually Duke of) Wellington in 1809, his many achievements in Iberia included the training of Portuguese units and their successful integration into divisions of the British Army; the establishment of the formidable defensive lines at Torres Vedras which protected Lisbon; and the groundwork laid for the offensive into Spain undertaken in 1812. Wellington maintained strict discipline within the ranks, in so doing establishing a first-rate, highly proficient fighting force which perfected methods for overpowering French columns through a combination of sustained musket fire and bayonet charges. After ousting French forces from Spain, he crossed

the frontier and took Toulouse, shortly after which the campaign ended when other Allied armies took Paris in March 1814. Wellington served as one of the British delegates at the Congress of Vienna in 1814–15, assuming command of Anglo-Allied forces in Belgium upon Napoleon's return from Elba.

*The duke in characteristic semi-civilian dress: a dark blue coat covered by a cloak and cape of the same colour, completed with a white neckcloth.*

Nor can Wellington's army be described as truly 'British', for it contained a mixture of nationalities, including Dutch and Belgian troops, many having fought for the French in recent years and whose loyalty therefore stood under suspicion. The fact that Wellington's command consisted of troops from across the Low Countries and parts of Germany gave rise to the term, 'Anglo-Allied Army', which represents a far more accurate description of his force than to refer to it simply as a 'British' army, since fewer than half his men hailed from across the Channel. Specifically, of the 73,200 troops under Wellington's command at Waterloo, only 36 per cent were British, with the remainder composed thusly: 10 per cent King's German Legion (KGL), i.e. Hanoverians in British service; 10 per cent Nassauer; 8 per cent Brunswicker; 17 per cent Hanoverian; 13 per cent Dutch; and 6 per cent Belgian. As a result approximately 45 per cent of the army spoke German as its primary language. The polyglot nature of the Anglo-Allied Army necessarily affected its quality, with the British and a particular portion of the duke's Hanoverian contingent constituting by far the better trained and more reliable troops. Hanoverians – north Germans – of two kinds fought at Waterloo: those, effectively raw militia, serving the re-established kingdom of Hanover by dint of the hereditary patrimony held by George III; and, by contrast, the highly reliable and competent troops of the King's German Legion – a component of the British Army – composed of volunteers who went into exile when the French invaded Hanover in 1803, supplemented two years later when a British expedition landed at the Elbe and Weser rivers, whereupon the ranks swelled and an *émigré* force keen to fight the French in any theatre of operations thereafter served very effectively in the Peninsula and southern France between 1808 and 1814. Finally, the tiny German states of Nassau and Brunswick supplied small contingents of their own. To compensate for the varying quality of this international force, Wellington reorganised his army along the pattern adopted in the Peninsula whereby he brigaded together formations of different nationalities with differing degrees of experience and training,

## Typical British Soldier

British soldiers tended to hail from the lowest social strata, though the popular image of recruits taking the king's shilling as an alternative to prison does not entirely stand up to scrutiny, for many gave up work as artisans, petty tradesmen, millers and agricultural workers. Nor did Wellington's oft-quoted condemnation of his men as the 'scum of the earth' actually represent his broad view of the common soldier – or indeed reflect anything more, when the remark is examined in its full context – than a criticism of those elements who drank to excess and looted. There is no denying that heavy drinking and outright drunkenness figured high amongst the vices characteristic of the common British soldier, who faced flogging as a consequence. A dozen lashes was not an uncommon sentence, though a man might endure many dozens at the whim of his colonel. The British soldier viewed this seemingly inordinately harsh practice with equanimity, for life in the army reflected life in society at large: imprisonment for debt, widespread criminality, no social welfare to speak of, hard living, a poor prospect of longevity, and little in the way of personal comforts. The common soldier intensely disliked arbitrary, unjustified or excessive punishments inflicted upon himself or his comrades, but not the practice of harsh punishment *per se*. So long as an officer used his power judiciously, with the punishment fitting the crime, his men respected his position of authority.

The British soldier was a particularly tough breed, for while he enjoyed a reputation for grumbling, he accepted his fate with resignation – and frequently with good humour. With proper training he ranked amongst the best soldiers in Europe. Certainly at Waterloo he was at least the equal of his French counterpart, with a stalwart attitude to defence and a keen readiness to engage his opponent once committed to the fray by the sword-wielding lieutenant of his platoon. Unlike his French counterpart, the British soldier was less willing overtly to express enthusiasm or anger; yet his quiet disposition belied a determination in battle which rendered him formidable indeed, particularly when skilled in the use of his musket, for whatever his shortcomings, no infantry in Europe could deliver a rate of fire to equal his.

# THE KING'S GERMAN LEGION

The King's German Legion, though a foreign corps, maintained a standard of discipline and training equal to that of British troops. They hailed from Hanover, most of their ranks formed in 1803 when the French overran the electorate but failed to prevent the Royal Navy from evacuating much of the Hanoverian Army to Britain. There, anxious to recover their country, the men eagerly enlisted in the service of George III, the third British monarch of the Hanoverian line. Comprised of units of all arms, the King's German Legion served loyally and very effectively throughout the Peninsular War and in the Waterloo campaign.

thereby stiffening divisions of otherwise green troops – such as the Dutch-Belgians – by mixing them with veteran British battalions.

In 1815, many of the veteran Prussian forces which had fought in the campaigns of 1813–14 to clear not only their own country but all of central Europe of French forces were back on home soil or had undergone reductions as a consequence of large-scale demobilisation. These measures seriously affected Prussia's state of preparedness, a circumstance exacerbated by financial problems which affected supply and equipment. Nevertheless, upon Napoleon's departure from Elba, King Frederick William III ordered the full-scale mobilisation of regular forces and called out the militia, known as the *Landwehr*, such that by the start of the campaign Field Marshal Blücher commanded just over 130,000 troops and 304 pieces of artillery, organised into four corps.

## Infantry Weapons and Tactics

More than 80 per cent of Napoleon's armies consisted of musket-armed infantry, organised into battalions with an average strength of 520 all ranks. The musket served as the basic weapon of the

*Marshal Blücher leading* landwehr *(militia) across the Rhine at the beginning of 1814. A veteran of the disastrous 1806 campaign in which the French first defeated the main Prussian field armies before proceeding to occupy Berlin and overrun the country, Blücher served as commander-in-chief of Prussian forces in what his countrymen called the 'War of German Liberation' which in 1813–14, in concert with the Russians and Austrians, first swept the French from central Europe before finally overcoming them on home soil.*

infantry, which was known as 'line' (in French, *ligne*) or 'foot' regiments owing to the ordinary functions they performed in the line of battle. Muskets were notoriously inaccurate; even a trained infantryman would be fortunate to strike his target at a hundred yards. His chances naturally increased as the distance shortened, which accounted for the regular exchange of volleys at 50–75 yards. Great destruction was caused at such ranges, or even when closer, which therefore left the advantage in the hands of better trained, better disciplined infantry, who typically fired by company or platoon when deployed in column or line. Light infantry (in French, *légère*), less heavily burdened with equipment and more agile on their feet, served most effectively when spread out as individual sharpshooters firing in a skirmish line as a screen for their formed compatriots, who stood shoulder to shoulder to maximise firepower and to facilitate the already difficult process of exercising command and control in an age of bugles, trumpets and shouting.

The muskets carried by the infantry of all nationalities at Waterloo were remarkably similar to one another. All consisted of a smooth bore (i.e. no specialised grooves producing a rifling effect) with a flintlock mechanism firing a lead ball of approximately an ounce in weight. Black powder served as the propellant, with the ball rammed down the muzzle. Any infantryman at Waterloo could load and fire a musket belonging to that of another nationality so long as he had the ammunition specific to that weapon. Thus, all that fundamentally distinguished muskets were their differing calibres, the Prussians using the Potsdam musket with a calibre of 19.5mm, his British ally the 18.7mm 'Brown Bess' and the French the 17.2mm Charleville. Firing a musket required a sequenced drill, which for British infantry consisted of eleven movements. Weight of fire – that is, the frequency with which an infantryman could discharge his musket – generally determined the victor, so long as one excludes other factors such as numbers or any role played by artillery or cavalry. All well-trained infantrymen could fire two, sometimes three shots a minute. The British generally achieved this rate of fire, while the French and Prussians probably fired two rounds per minute at best.

Space precludes discussion of all types of muskets, but the bare specifications of the 'India Pattern' musket, better known as the 'Brown Bess', carried by British infantry provides a general impression. Its 39in. barrel accommodated a triangular 17in. spike bayonet, the whole weapon weighing 11lbs. Soldiers carried sixty cartridges consisting of greased paper packets containing ball and powder. Two battalions of British infantry and a number of their German allies carried rifles of various kinds. The Baker rifle, carried by the 95th Regiment, enjoyed a considerably longer range than a musket – 200 yards or more – though this advantage came at the expense of a slower loading process than that required of a Brown Bess. The grooved barrel which twisted the ball and thus provided greater stability accounted for the rifle's increased range of accuracy. On the other hand, the rifle was less robust than the musket, more expensive to manufacture and required far more practice to master; hence, the British Army's reliance on the musket as the standard infantry weapon.

As a close-order weapon, the bayonet saw less use than popularly believed, although the bitter fighting in and around the fortified structures of Hougoumont and La Haie Sainte as well as in the village of Plancenoit to the southeast saw its extensive use. The bayonet's principal benefit lay in its psychological effect since infantry and cavalry generally did not charge into the defensive hedge of steel thus created and only steady troops were likely to stand up to a determined attack by infantry advancing with the bayonet at the ready. Instead, a unit normally only charged with the bayonet once its intended target began to waver as a consequence of heavy losses inflicted by musket or artillery fire. The approach of an enemy, shouting menacingly and advancing at a rapid pace with bayonets levelled, tended to drive off untried or unsteady defenders before a clash of steel ever took place.

As the Anglo-Allies stood on the defensive during the entire course of the battle, their tactics naturally reflected this circumstance. Many units remained more or less in the same position for much or all of the fighting since Wellington required them simply to hold the ground on which they stood. Tactics were based on fire and movement, the first to inflict casualties on the enemy and the second to place units in a position in which to fire. Infantry which could deliver two or three shots a minute and alter formation efficiently stood a good chance of success at Waterloo. Anglo-Allied infantry were organised around the battalion as the basic fighting unit (itself sub-divided into companies) with an average strength at Waterloo of 640 all ranks, 615 for the Prussians. When deployed in line the battalion stood in two ranks, which allowed every weapon to bear on a target at any one time, whereas the French and Prussians fought in ranks of three, whose advantage lay in the narrower frontage and ease of manoeuvre.

*Hand-to-hand combat between British light infantry and French grenadiers at Waterloo. While they carried the same weapons as their counterparts in ordinary line regiments, light infantry received training in order to operate in extended order as skirmishers. Grenadiers had by this time long since abandoned use of the grenade, but still retained their élite status.*

Infantry adopted one of three tactical formations: column, line and square. Each offered benefits and drawbacks, leaving officers to decide which formation to adopt and when to execute the various drills required to alter their unit's formation in order to meet a specific requirement in attack or defence. Adopting the correct formation and choosing the timing when circumstances dictated such change could profoundly affect unit effectiveness – or even its survival on the battlefield. By dint of its extended frontage, the line offered the greatest firepower, though space might preclude its feasibility. The column was employed for speed of movement or when circumstances did not immediately reveal the best formation required, since infantry could change formation from column to line or to square with relative ease. The square, by which infantry established an all-round defence in four ranks with all sides facing outwards, offered the best protection against cavalry.

The column offered a narrow front and substantial depth and enabled an attacker so deployed to concentrate its force to drive off a defender. At Waterloo, French columns stood with a frontage of about 200 yards. While rapid movement towards the enemy – thus subjecting the men in this formation to less time under fire – bestowed certain virtues, failure to prepare the target with sufficient fire by artillery and skirmishers generally left the column unable to dislodge the object of its attack. Moreover, once a column moved it could not fire, and success depended much more on the fire of, for instance, artillery in a supporting role to enable the infantry to drive off the defender. As proved repeatedly in the Peninsula, when French artillery or clouds of skirmishers failed to inflict heavy casualties on British infantry prior to an attack in column, the assault invariably foundered under the withering fire of the defender.

The square, although difficult to form, rendered itself all but impervious to cavalry by presenting on all sides an impenetrable hedge of bayonets. On the other hand, thus deployed, the battalion found its firepower greatly reduced since many fewer of its soldiers could bring their weapons to bear. Moreover, where enemy infantry or artillery lay close at hand, the square found itself extremely vulnerable, since its reduced firepower, inability to move at any appreciable speed and, above all, its compactness rendered it a prime target for artillery. Tight ranks were critical to a square's survival against cavalry, but if attacking horsemen benefitted from supporting artillery, infantry in square endured terrible punishment and could in theory be driven off, leaving the fleeing infantry at the mercy of pursuing horsemen.

## Cavalry Weapons and Tactics

As with infantry, cavalry in the three armies at Waterloo were effectively clothed and armed in a similar fashion to one another and fought using largely similar weapons and tactics. Light cavalry, such as hussars, chasseurs, light dragoons and lancers tended to

*French cuirassiers formed up in a two-rank line. Large men mounted on large horses, cuirassiers served as heavy cavalry, with the charge their raison d'être. Their long, heavy, straight sabres were designed for thrusting, with the arm extended forward so as to drive the sharp point into an opponent in contrast to the swinging slash employed by the light cavalry, which wielded curved sabres.*

perform a reconnaissance role, screened the army's movement from the enemy and pursued the defeated foe. Medium cavalry, almost exclusively classed as dragoons, carried out the charge in battle. Heavy cavalry, which in the French Army consisted of helmeted and breast-plated cuirassiers and carabiniers, served as the principal shock weapon, often kept in reserve to deliver a great, decisive blow.

Private Smithies of the (British) 1st Dragoon Guards recorded this account of hand-to-hand fighting with cuirassiers:

The cuirassiers, you will recollect, had coats of steel, whilst we had no such protection; and then again their swords were much longer... On we rushed at each other, and when we met the shock was terrific. We wedged ourselves between them as much as possible, to prevent them from cutting, and the noise of the horses, the clashing of swords against their steel armour, can be imagined only by those who heard it. There were some riders who had caught hold of each other's bodies – wrestling fashion – and fighting for life, but the superior physical strength of our regiment soon showed itself… It was desperate work indeed, cutting through their steel armour…

Adkin, The Waterloo Companion, p.220

As cavalry cannot hold ground like infantry, its only means of defence is to attack. Standing to receive a charge surrendered impetus to the enemy and almost invariably led to defeat. Even light cavalry therefore operated on the basis that it must use the weight and momentum of its movement – even if not actually charging – to achieve some sort of success over an opponent, whether mounted or otherwise. The charge proceeded at a gradually increasing rate of advance, starting from about 600 paces at a trot, rising to a canter at 400, to a gallop at 150 paces, and the final rush at 50 paces. Cavalry carried swords, sabres or lances, depending on the type and function of the regiment. Heavy cavalry wielded a long, heavy straight sword with both edges and its point sharpened. Light cavalry carried a light, curved weapon known as a sabre. They also carried a firearm, usually a pistol or carbine, the latter a lighter and shorter version of an infantryman's musket – though these were virtually useless except at extremely close range.

The regiment, sub-divided into squadrons formed the basic tactical unit for cavalry, with an average strength for both French and Anglo-Allied regiments of 460 all ranks. Tactics and formation varied depending on circumstances. Ideally, cavalry hoped to catch infantry unprepared to receive them – especially skirmishers, who possessed virtually no defence against formed cavalry; but more usually they might also strike a column or line, or a battery of guns. At Waterloo, fully fledged charges at a gallop or better were rare owing to the confined space caused by the very high density

# CAVALRY RATES OF MOVEMENT

A walking horse covers little more ground than a foot soldier. At a walk, a cavalry regiment moving along an unimpeded road or track covers about 4km in an hour – marginally further than an infantry unit. At a brisk walk horsemen cover about 6km, rising to 10km at a forced march pace.

*French lancers charging at Waterloo. Nearly all European armies fielded lancer regiments, with the British a notable exception. In wet weather, as at Quatre Bras, the lance proved a highly destructive weapon, for its length enabled the bearer to spear an infantryman while beyond the reach of the bayonet and achieve the same result against a mounted opponent armed with a sword. On the other hand, the lancer stood nearly defenceless if his adversary parried the point and provided a counter-thrust.*

of combatants. This is not to assert that cavalry did not attack; they frequently did, but seldom did they carry out an assault at great speed, especially considering the various obstacles that stood in their way, including troops, guns, ammunition wagons, sunken roads, hedges, slopes, and wet ground. In most instances cavalry at Waterloo seldom advanced more quickly than at a trot, operating most effectively when accompanied by horse artillery, which usually consisted of batteries of six 6-pounders which moved into the best possible position of support before unlimbering and bombarding a particular target, hopefully causing it to waver or, better still, break just before the cavalry pressed home its attack, thus enabling the horsemen to inflict maximum casualties on a unit incapable of offering a proper defence.

In action cavalry tended to restrict itself to two basic formations: the column and the line. Circumstances dictated their use and a regiment very much depended on the skill of its commander to choose the most suitable formation, which was often based on such factors as the enemy's formation, the space available to deploy the unit and timing. Cavalry experienced many of the same benefits and drawbacks as infantry deployed in like formation. The column facilitated quick movement since it was easier to control than a line, which required constant dressing to keep the ranks from becoming ragged. Mounted units in column also suffered from fewer problems when encountering obstacles and, owing to their narrower frontage, left the enemy ignorant of their strength unless they could be viewed from an elevated position. The column also enabled a regiment to deploy quickly into the formation most popularly used in the attack: the line, which owing to its narrower depth left the regiment less vulnerable to artillery fire as it approached its target and positioned the largest possible number of troopers on the broadest possible front. The column had the disadvantage of being particularly vulnerable to artillery fire, since while its density and depth furnished it greater 'shock' value than a line, it effectively guaranteed that a round shot would wreak havoc against file after file of man and horse.

## Artillery

Artillery at Waterloo varied in type according to the armies involved but, again as with the others arms – infantry and cavalry – it did not

# CAVALRY FRONTAGES

A mounted cavalry troop occupied a metre of frontage.
Thus, a regiment consisting of three squadrons each
of 150 men would measure about 70m across when
formed up in column of squadrons with each squadron
arrayed in two ranks. If deployed in line, an equal
number of horsemen occupied a frontage of more than
200m – and thus presented both an impressive sight
and an easy target for enemy artillery.

*Napoleon personally sighting a gun – in this case at Montereau, during
the 1814 campaign in France. Originally trained as a gunner, the emperor
appreciated better than all his contemporaries the critical importance of
artillery in battle, particularly when well served by gun crews who could
operate in a combined arms context; that is, closely coordinating their
firepower with infantry and cavalry attacks.*

differ substantially in technological terms from one army to another.
Heavy guns provided greater striking power, which meant that a
heavier ball travelled further, losing its kinetic energy at a slower

43

rate than its lighter calibre counterpart. Guns were organised into batteries, generally of six pieces. Like small arms, guns were smooth-bore and muzzle-loading, with the type of gun identified by the weight of the shot it fired; hence, a 6-pounder fired a 6lb iron shot. A gun (technically, not referred to by contemporaries as 'cannon') fired with direct line of sight, which required that the crew actually see the target, as opposed to the howitzer, an indirect fire weapon which lobbed its ordnance over the crests of slopes or garden walls in a high trajectory so that the projectile's timed fuse exploded above or on its target, sending fragments of shell in all directions. This was in contrast to the traditional and much more widely used round shot, which consisted of a simple iron sphere which smashed its way through ranks of man and beast alike.

Range depended on the size of shot but, for instance, a Prussian 6-pounder could project its shot a maximum range of 1,500m, though its most effective range consisted of about half that distance. A British 6-pounder's most effective range fell between 600m and 700m, while a French 12-pounder could fire as far as 1,800m, but ideally struck its target at half that distance. Anti-personnel ammunition, such as canister shot, consisted of a thin tin container filled with lead balls which upon leaving the barrel spread with the effect of a giant shotgun, though the inaccuracy of this method meant that this form of ammunition could only be used at the closest ranges. Thus, a French 6-pounder firing

## DISABLING UNCREWED GUNS

The most common way to disable a captured piece of artillery was effected by driving a headless, tapered steel spike down the vent near the base of the barrel. While the spike could later be removed, this was not possible in the heat of battle and thus denied the enemy the use of a gun even if recovered from temporary loss or under circumstances in which the shortage of time prevented its being drawn away.

# SHRAPNEL

The British were the only army to use shrapnel, which consisted of a hollow iron sphere filled with musket balls and gunpowder ignited by a fuse. As success depended on it bursting in the air at precisely the right trajectory and time – thus showering its target beyond musket range – it required a highly skilled crew to make effective use of it.

canister enjoyed a range of 400–450m; a British 9-pounder 450m and a Prussian 12-pounder 550m. Canister shot caused horrific damage to targets at such ranges, particularly attacking columns of infantry or cavalry or, above all, squares of static infantry which, if positioned beyond 150 yards, posed no danger to the gunners, who could pummel a square pinned in position by the nearby presence of cavalry. On the other hand, artillery crews stood no chance against cavalry if they found their batteries overrun, and thus depended on reaching the safety of nearby infantry if they chose to abandon their guns until the danger passed.

Despite all that may be said about the soft ground at Waterloo impeding the progress of round shot on its first contact with the ground, eyewitness accounts abound with stories of heavy losses and horrendous injuries inflicted by artillery, particularly by the French, who brought 246 pieces to the field, as opposed to Wellington's 157 and the Prussians' (eventual) 134. Ensign Keppel, a 16-year-old in the 14th Foot, observed the fate of a bugler of the 51st Foot thus:

> ... a round shot took off his head and spattered the whole battalion [deployed in square] with his brains, the colours and the ensigns in charge of them coming in for an extra share. One of them, Charles Fraser, a fine gentleman in speech and manner, raised a laugh by drawling out, 'How extremely disgusting!' A second shot carried off six of the men's bayonets, a third broke

the breastbone of a Lance-Sergeant, whose piteous cries were anything but encouraging to his youthful comrades.

Adkin, p.263

So intense, in fact, proved the French bombardment of Wellington's centre, that some of the duke's less steady units, like the Brunswickers, were visibly shaken and nearly broke and ran under fire. Captain Mercer, commander of 'G' troop, Royal Artillery, witnessed the effect of French artillery on a nearby square of his German allies:

The Brunswickers were falling fast – the shot every moment making great gaps in their squares, which the officers and sergeants were actively employed in filling up by pushing their men together, and sometimes thumping them 'ere they could make them move… Today they fled not bodily, to be sure, but spiritually, for their senses seemed to have left them. There they stood with recovered arms, like so many logs, or rather like the very wooden figures I had seen them practising at in their cantonments. Every moment I feared they would again throw down their arms and flee: but their officers and sergeants behaved nobly, not only keeping them together, but managing to keep their squares closed in spite of the carnage made amongst them.

## TRANSPARENT COWARDICE

The Cumberland Hussars, a Hanoverian unit with British officers, unaccountably abandoned the field in the midst of the battle despite orders to advance. When challenged, their commander, Lieutenant Colonel Hake stated that his men were all volunteers, had provided their own mounts and that he possessed little confidence in their abilities. The unit then proceeded rapidly to Brussels where the men caused a panic by claiming the French had won the battle and were *en route* for Brussels.

# THE DAYS
# BEFORE BATTLE

## Napoleon Returns to Power

Napoleon had never been resigned to managing the internal affairs of Elba – hardly surprising for a man who had controlled a vast empire and dreamed of pursuing his destiny once again. Determined to return to power, he sailed for France on the evening of 26 February, accompanied by a small flotilla and about 1,100 soldiers – all loyal followers who had remained with him on Elba. Three vessels, one French and the others British, failed to detect Napoleon, who landed on 1 March near Antibes, where the garrison offered no resistance. He then proceeded north, gathering adherents as he went, particularly at Laffrey, where a whole regiment defected to his cause, leaving the Bourbon authorities in Paris paralysed by a situation in which the army revealed its true allegiances by refusing to stop the usurper's progress towards the capital. At Lyon, thought to be a royalist stronghold, support for the king faltered and the city welcomed the prodigal emperor, thereby increasing his forces still further. Marshal Ney, one of the greatest commanders of the imperial years but now in royal employ, initially pledged to capture the 'Corsican ogre' and return him to Paris in a cage; but, like thousands of others, he cast aside his allegiance to the king and gave further impetus to Napoleonic momentum. Thus, entering

## Marshal Michel Ney (1769–1815)

Charismatic, courageous, temperamental, passionate, quick-tempered, brilliant and brave beyond question, Ney was so determined to place himself in the thick of battle at Waterloo that he denied the army the 'eyes and ears' of its *de facto* battlefield commander, thereby allowing events to move beyond his immediate control. Ney doubtless inspired his troops in the assault, but in so doing reduced himself at best to another corps – or probably more accurately, a divisional or even brigade – commander. Possessing brash manners and displaying unpredictable behaviour, he was not entirely trusted by a number of generals during the campaign of 1815 – and perhaps for good reason – for after boasting that he would bring Napoleon home in a cage, Ney famously changed sides, a problem highlighted by the fact that he had only held command for three days before Waterloo and therefore did not know his subordinates, many of whom resented his sudden appointment. Unlike Napoleon, Ney possessed personal experience of confronting Wellington, having served in the Peninsula for three years, most notably in 1810 at Busaco where he rashly launched his forces against a well-defended and formidable ridge. But he later served brilliantly in Russia and Germany until, after Allied forces occupied Paris in April 1814 and thus rendered all hope of further resistance futile, he led a group of marshals who insisted upon Napoleon's abdication. When the emperor refused, declaring 'The Army will obey me!', Ney disarmed him with a flourish of reality: 'Sire, the Army will obey its generals'. During the Hundred Days' campaign Ney committed a number of mistakes at Quatre Bras, attacking late, launching attacks in piecemeal fashion and failing to use combined arms to break Anglo-Allied resistance.

*Marshal Michel Ney. Proud and argumentative, over the course of more than twenty-five years in the army he frequently bickered with fellow officers on matters both tactical and strategic.*

the Tuileries Palace in triumph on 20 March, without so much as a shot being fired to oppose him, the emperor re-established political and military authority over most of the country with minimal objection, apart from the Vendée and traditional royalist parts of the south, where troops suppressed the uprising in the former while the advance of Napoleonic forces against Marseille and Toulon brought them to heel without recourse to violence. There appeared a certain inevitability to the whole course of events, for Louis had accomplished little to attract popularity in the brief period of the Restoration and failed to summon the arguments required to oppose the return of a man whose promises to protect France from external threats met with wide approval.

Napoleon ensured his popularity by promising reforms meant to reverse some of the reactionary measures implemented by the Bourbons. He abolished feudal titles and authorised public works, promised constitutional government in the style of the 1790s and liberal concessions like freedom of the press and the preservation of the constitutional assemblies established by Louis, but on a more democratic basis. At the same time, Napoleon hoped to placate the crowned heads of Europe whose forces were on the march with the expressed intention of removing him from the throne. He promised to honour existing treaties and declared himself committed to peaceful co-existence with all Europe. All the while, however, he put out diplomatic feelers to some of the minor states of Iberia, Germany and Italy in pursuit of allies, appealing as well to foreigners who had served the Napoleonic cause to return to the fold.

## Opposing Strategies

None of the Allied forces which had taken Paris and deposed Napoleon in 1814 remained in France, but the diplomats, still assembled at Vienna and tasked with forging a political and territorial settlement for Europe, appreciated the necessity of setting aside their differences – particularly over the question of allocating Polish and Saxon territory to Russia and Prussia, respectively. On 13 March the Allies duly declared Napoleon an outlaw, with no legitimate claim to the French crown, and offered help to Louis XVIII. Two days later Lord Liverpool's government summoned the Duke of Wellington, acting on behalf of Britain, back from Vienna to assume command of the Anglo-Allied forces in Belgium. On the 25th the major European powers represented at the Austrian capital, together with many minor powers besides, and resuscitated the alliance of 1814, with Austria, Prussia, Russia and Britain each committing 150,000 men to the coming campaign, with the caveat that Britain could supply a smaller force in return for subsidies paid to other powers who could furnish proportionally greater numbers of troops. In the event, units from some of the minor German states who joined this, the Seventh Coalition, pledged themselves to serve under Wellington's command.

All told, the Allies mustered 700,000 troops, but most of these, consisting of Austrians and Russians, required months to reach France. The only Allied forces immediately available stood in Belgium, consisting of 95,000 British, Dutch-Belgian and Hanoverian troops under the Prince of Orange in the west and 120,000 Prussians under Lieutenant General Gneisenau in the valley of the Meuse to the east. Wellington maintained that the campaign should open once the Allies could field 450,000 men, confident that Napoleon could deploy no more than a third of that number. The emperor, for his part, reckoned that time was of the essence; if he was to succeed against superior numbers his only chance lay in striking first, defeating the separate elements of the Allies' forces in Belgium before the overwhelming numbers *en route* for the Rhine could be brought to bear against him. Whereas the bulk of his opponents' forces still lay far to the east, operating on exterior lines of communication, French troops could operate close to home soil with the added benefit of the geographical protection partly afforded by the Alps and Pyrenees. By launching an offensive, moreover, Napoleon hoped to galvanise domestic political support, forestall opposition in Paris and disrupt the coalition ranged against him. In short, if he could defeat the Allies in detail, there stood a reasonable prospect of disabling the coalition altogether while consolidating his hold at home.

Strategically, the key to French success required local superiority in numbers, without exposing Paris. Striking east into Germany against the slowly approaching Austrians and Russians would not offer Napoleon such advantages, for his forces remained relatively small and the proximity of the Anglo-Allies and Prussians to the north offered them the opportunity to threaten Napoleon's left flank as well as the French capital. Thus, military logic dictated that the emperor strike north, into Belgium, with all possible speed.

Wellington arrived in Brussels on 4 April and assumed command of Anglo-Allied forces, thus succeeding the Prince of Orange. Unable in the short term to rely on aid from the Russians and Austrians, the Allied armies in Belgium (now, formally, the United Netherlands, which included Holland) necessarily adopted a defensive posture. Ignorance of the probable axis of French advance moreover obliged the Allies to deploy their forces over a wide area of Belgium, a task complicated by the large number of roads, paved and unpaved, available to the French, not only on the line of march south of the border, but in southern Belgium as well, particularly via Lille. Such routes led to key cities like Antwerp, Brussels, Ostend and Ghent, any one of which the French might have good reason to capture. The Allies' conundrum lay in the fact that they could not defend them all simultaneously, and indeed covering more than one left the Allies dangerously dispersed. Anticipating French objectives proved problematical: both Ostend and Antwerp provided vital lines of communication across the Channel for Wellington; Ghent constituted the refuge of the exiled court of Louis XVIII, whom the Allies pledged to protect; Brussels, as the capital of Belgium, represented a key strategic position of much psychological value, particularly in light of the dubious allegiance of the Dutch-Belgian troops, many of whom

## WELLINGTON'S HABITS AND CHARACTER

Detached and inaccessible, if the duke did not enjoy his soldier's affections he certainly earned their respect – and for sound reasons. Always present to lend an air of calm and to set an example of steadiness during a crisis in battle, he invariably issued prompt, exact, laconic orders and seldom spoke except to issue a command. Oblivious to shot and shell, the duke displayed no concern for his own safety. Proof of his regular presence near the frontline manifested itself in stark terms, for more than half of his staff officers were killed or wounded during the course of the day. Wellington disliked delegating responsibility to subordinates when he could handle a matter personally. Unlike nearly all his subordinates, the duke shunned the ostentation of senior officer's dress, preferring to wear a simple, unadorned cocked hat, blue frock coat and cape. Nor did he insist on smartness within the ranks. Rather, he demanded a high state of fighting discipline and proficiency in musket fire, since the principal ingredient of success in battle lay in a unit's ability to stand fast while delivering – as well as receiving – fire.

had previously served Napoleon; and the fortresses along the Meuse, notably Namur, Liège and Maastricht, provided protection to the Low Countries against invasion.

Yet despite each city's inherent merits, the capture of all such places lay subordinate to Napoleon's prime objective: the defeat in succession of the two Allied armies, in whichever order circumstances dictated. In turn, the Allies' success could be measured in terms of their ability to maintain their forces operationally viable – that is, effectively intact and capable of fighting – thus denying Napoleon the separate victories he required before the massive Russian and Austrian armies could bring their truly palpable force to bear. In short, both sides understood two fundamental points: first, the existence of the Allied armies represented their centre of gravity; and second, their preservation depended on their uniting or, at the very least, operating on a co-operative basis, thus preventing the French from isolating and defeating them in succession. It was therefore incumbent upon the two Allied commanders to ascertain as quickly as possible the French axis of advance and respond accordingly, concentrating their forces so as to engage Napoleon with superior numbers.

From the outset Wellington and Blücher proposed different strategies for the campaign, the former advocating deployment south of Brussels and the latter wishing to shift all forces to Tirlemont, approximately 25 miles east of Brussels, thus connecting the Prussians more closely to their logistical tail; that is, their lines of supply. The duke opposed the idea on the grounds that it would expose Brussels to French occupation, thus imperilling Britain's alliance with the Netherlands and risking the defection of the latter's politically suspect forces. Moreover, the fall of the capital would sever Wellington's links with Ostend – his line of communication across the Channel – and open the way to the vital port of Antwerp. Gneisenau, the temporary commander of Prussian forces while he awaited Blücher's arrival, bowed to the duke's objections; accordingly, the two armies – with Wellington's by mid-June increased to approximately 112,000 troops, of whom just over 90,000 served in the field army – proceeded on separate routes to positions south of Brussels, in so doing placing his forces closer to the French border and therefore exposing them to more immediate contact with Napoleon's *Armée du Nord* – a circumstance beneficial only if the Allies could concentrate beforehand lest they risk separation and defeat in detail. Yet, doing so – concentrating components within their respective armies as well as uniting as a whole – required their moving across the path of Napoleon's thrust northwards. The Allies therefore would merely await Napoleon, who intended to occupy a central position, from there defeating the two Allied armies separately before taking Brussels. In the event, the Prussian I Corps occupied a position which blocked the road to Brussels via Charleroi – the route of advance Napoleon chose.

# Field Marshal Gebhard Leberecht von Blücher

Aggressive, excessively driven, hard-drinking and affable, Blücher displayed more the traits of an NCO than of an officer – much less a field marshal. Yet he was the right man for the job: Prussia needed an offensive-minded commander-in-chief during the years 1813–15 and Blücher deserves considerable credit for honouring his promise to assist Wellington during the Waterloo campaign. In light of the Prussians' severe mauling at Ligny, the determination of the man becomes all the more apparent. Blücher began his military service in the 1750s, serving in the Seven Years War (1756–63) and later in the Revolutionary Wars, mostly on the Rhine. He commanded a cavalry corps under the Duke of Brunswick during Prussia's ill-fated campaign of 1806, in which Blücher displayed an ill-advised, impetuous keenness to attack at Auerstädt, so contributing to Count Hohenlohe's abject defeat. Undaunted, he not only held the line to enable the bulk of the army to retreat, but managed through sheer force of character and a driving will to lead 22,000 survivors to Lübeck, on the Baltic coast, earning the eternal admiration of his countrymen in his capacity as the last Prussian field commander to capitulate to the French, for whom Blücher possessed a particular loathing – a view he openly expressed. As a consequence, during the long period of his country's occupation – formalised by the Treaty of Tilsit in July 1807, Blücher was deliberately excluded from senior command. When King Frederick William III joined the Sixth Coalition in early 1813, Blücher enthusiastically accepted command of Prussian forces and,

despite suffering initial defeats at Lützen and Bautzen, pressed on remorselessly to participate in the colossal struggle at Leipzig. He played an instrumental role in numerous engagements during the campaign in France which followed, confirming throughout these years his reputation as an inspirational leader.

*Despite being 72 in 1815, Blücher exhibited boundless energy, prompting his men to nickname him 'Marschall Vorwärts' ('Marshal Forwards') in recognition of his relentless commitment to offensive action.*

## Opening Moves

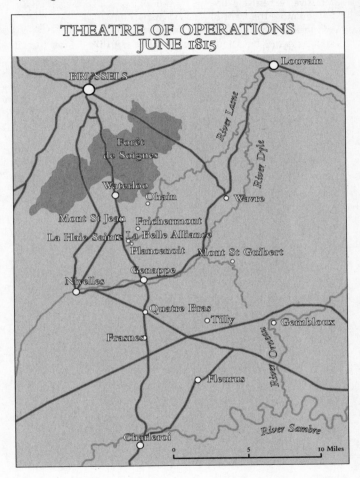

THEATRE OF OPERATIONS
JUNE 1815

Without intelligence of enemy movements in northern France, the Allies remained ignorant of the axis of principal attack and consequently found themselves caught partly by surprise, notwithstanding the fact that Blücher (replacing Gneisenau, who remained as Chief of Staff) knew – partly as a consequence of the defection of General Bourmont, a divisional commander – that the French were concentrating forces southwest of Charleroi. As it happened, Bourmont's supposition that the Prussians could expect to be attacked on the morning of 15 June proved correct; before dawn on the 15th the French crossed the frontier and descended upon Charleroi, straddling the river Sambre and held by a small Prussian force. Strongly outnumbered, the Prussians briefly defended the bridge before withdrawing, losing about 2,000 men in the affair and leaving the French, with 600 casualties, in possession of the town and the way north clear. Meanwhile, Ziethen, commander of I Corps retreated in order to concentrate with other formations and to avoid substantial losses. Simultaneously, II and III Corps moved to oppose the French advance, while Wellington, as yet unaware of the direction of Napoleon's main thrust – and erroneously predicting an advance further west, via Mons – failed to react promptly, despite receiving word from Ziethen, via Major General von Müffling, the Prussian military liaison officer at Wellington's headquarters, of the French advance through Charleroi and the direction of their subsequent advance. Having promised Blücher on 3 June to shift his forces towards the Prussians in the event of French attack, Wellington now failed to do so in a timely manner, thus throwing into doubt the possibility of the Allies linking up and opposing Napoleon together.

While the Allies sought to take up mutually supporting positions south of Brussels, Marshal Ney, commanding the French left wing, sought out Wellington by moving north from Charleroi along the Brussels road, an advance which lacked the eagerness to engage the enemy so characteristic of the marshal's previous years in command. As a consequence, he failed to seize the important crossroads of Quatre Bras, 2 miles north of Charleroi, partly owing to the lacklustre manner in which he sought to clear the road of a small blocking force of Nassauers at Frasnes. Nevertheless, by nightfall on the 15th Napoleon had managed to interpose his forces between those of Wellington and Blücher, leaving both to be engaged separately, with the duke's forces yet to concentrate. Had he been in a position to strike these scattered forces on the 15th, Napoleon might have prevented Wellington from establishing any substantial field force; but faulty administration by Marshal Soult, the Chief of Staff, resulted in much of the emperor's forces remaining on the wrong side of the Sambre by evening, thereby preventing Napoleon from profiting by Wellington's own difficulties in assembling his scattered forces.

By way of rectifying his vulnerable position – all the more so once news arrived of Napoleon's close proximity, while he and his officers attended the Duchess of Richmond's ball in Brussels on the night of the 15th – Wellington ordered the whole of his forces to converge on the crossroads at Quatre Bras, a place from which he could both block the route to the capital and either move to assist the Prussians if the French attacked Blücher or, conversely, to benefit from the Prussians' presence in the event the French attacked the Anglo-Allies. With this in mind, on the afternoon of the 16th both commanders met, the duke offering to aid Blücher with 20,000 men if the French engaged the Prussians, provided of course that the Anglo-Allies had not themselves encountered a substantial body of the enemy. In fact, such a promise was rather disingenuous, not because Ney actually attacked him later that day and therefore spared him from honouring his promise, but on the grounds that Wellington misled his Prussian counterpart by failing to admit that many Anglo-Allied formations remained scattered – and indeed would remain so for most of the 16th. In the event, Napoleon chose to attack both Allied armies simultaneously, sending Ney with the left wing to confront Wellington at Quatre Bras while the emperor engaged the Prussians at the village of Ligny, where Blücher concentrated three out of his four corps.

Action commenced around 2.30pm, with the Prussians foolishly deployed on a forward slope, thereby exposing them to devastating French artillery fire. Still, with 93,000 men against 66,000 – an advantage of one-third – they could endure heavy

*Napoleon, accompanied by his staff, at Ligny, where while he badly defeated the Prussians, he nevertheless failed to ensure that they could not link up with the Anglo-Allies two days later at Waterloo. In the foreground dragoons prepare to charge.*

losses, but owing to vaguely worded orders the Prussian IV Corps, under Bülow, failed to join the main body and thus played no part at Ligny, where their absence was keenly felt. Still, Napoleon suffered from his own problems of concentration, including the failure to make use of VI Corps, under *Comte* Lobau, who arrived late to the fighting. Worse still, when both Ney and Napoleon ordered *Comte* d'Erlon's I Corps to march to their assistance, the resulting confusion left the exasperated commander unable to appear at either battlefield. Accordingly, lacking the manpower he required to turn Blücher's right flank, Napoleon simply launched his troops forward in a series of expensive frontal assaults which resulted in separate, desperate struggles to seize and hold the village, whose fate shifted as each side ejected the other in succession at great cost to both combatants. By nightfall, largely thanks to coordinated efforts by artillery and cavalry against the Prussian centre, the French at last drove their opponents from

*General Friedrich von Bülow, commander of the Prussian IV Corps. Arriving piecemeal on the Waterloo battlefield, his men immediately engaged the French despite a wet and difficult 17km march from Dion le Mont, southeast of Wavre. Bülow's 14th Brigade fought a bitter hand-to-hand contest with the Young Guard for possession of the graveyard in Plancenoit, which changed hands several times – a testament to the vicious and desperate nature of the fighting there.*

the field – but not without receiving, as well as inflicting, heavy casualties, with 13,700 French killed and wounded as compared to 18,800 Prussians. Vitally, the Prussians – though badly mauled, with their commander bruised after a fall from his horse under which he lay trapped for some minutes – managed to extricate themselves from the field intact, so enabling them to remain a force in being. In this respect, though Ligny constituted a tactical victory for the French, it represented at the same time a strategic defeat, for the Prussians stood ready, after a brief period of recovery, to fight another day – a situation which, two days later at Waterloo, Napoleon thought unlikely though not altogether out of the question.

*Lieutenant General Sir Thomas Picton. He served in the abortive campaign on the island of Walcheren, off the Dutch coast, in 1809 before taking command of the hard-fighting 3rd Division in the Peninsula the following year. At its head he fought at Busaco (1810), the Lines of Torres Vedras (1810), Fuentes de Oñoro (1811) and the sieges of Ciudad Rodrigo and Badajoz (1812), at the last of which he was seriously wounded. On recovering, Picton returned to Spain and led his division at Vitoria (1813), which sealed the fate of French ambitions in Spain. Wounded again at Quatre Bras, he was killed at Waterloo during a French counterattack.*

At precisely the time Napoleon launched his attack against Blücher at Ligny, Ney pressed forward against Wellington only 6 miles to the northwest at Quatre Bras. At the outset the French marshal enjoyed a healthy *initial* numerical advantage of 28,000 to only 8,000 Anglo-Allies, for the duke not only had issued his orders for concentration very late on the 15th, but himself set out late from Brussels on the morning of the 16th with the forces he commanded there. As a consequence, he spent the afternoon perilously fending off waves of French attacks as more and more friendly formations filtered on to the battlefield. In the meantime, especially before Sir Thomas Picton's 5th Division reached the

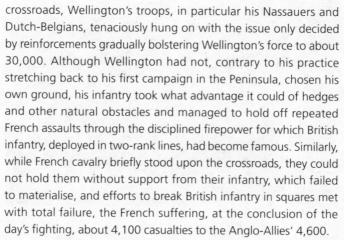

## WELLINGTON'S CHOICE OF BATTLEGROUND

The area of operations south of Brussels was surveyed by the Royal Engineers who, on Wellington's instructions, hurriedly prepared a map which in the event measured 4ft by 3ft and reached the duke at Quatre Bras. On it he sketched out the defensive lines he intended to draw up just south of the village of Waterloo. The map became soaked in blood while in the possession of the quartermaster general, Sir William De Lancey, who was mortally wounded in the battle. Wellington had himself first seen service in the Low Countries in the 1790s, re-acquainting himself with the probable theatre of operations once he reached Brussels from Vienna.

crossroads, Wellington's troops, in particular his Nassauers and Dutch-Belgians, tenaciously hung on with the issue only decided by reinforcements gradually bolstering Wellington's force to about 30,000. Although Wellington had not, contrary to his practice stretching back to his first campaign in the Peninsula, chosen his own ground, his infantry took what advantage it could of hedges and other natural obstacles and managed to hold off repeated French assaults through the disciplined firepower for which British infantry, deployed in two-rank lines, had become famous. Similarly, while French cavalry briefly stood upon the crossroads, they could not hold them without support from their infantry, which failed to materialise, and efforts to break British infantry in squares met with total failure, the French suffering, at the conclusion of the day's fighting, about 4,100 casualties to the Anglo-Allies' 4,600.

Much of the French failure to break Wellington's tenuous hold on the crossroads may be attributed to the absence of I Corps. While Allied units arrived piecemeal, hastily deployed and fed themselves into the battle the moment they arrived, what Ney needed most was the additional 20,000 men composing d'Erlon's absent formation. To Ney's extreme aggravation, Napoleon had overridden his plea for assistance, the emperor instead insisting that I Corps operate against the Prussian right flank at Ligny, so withholding from Ney the numbers which might very well have driven Wellington from his position and denied him the ability to take up a far more defensible one near Waterloo two days later. Napoleon's plan for Ney to rapidly defeat Wellington before aiding the emperor at Ligny on the same day also went awry, not only owing to the late dispatch of orders to this effect, but, again, by the emperor's robbing Ney of d'Erlon's men. Ironically, through this astonishing mismanagement and confusion, I Corps reached neither battlefield on the 16th and consequently left Napoleon little option but to abandon any notion of outflanking Blücher and instead to rely on the more costly alternative of direct assaults and

*Napoleon at Ligny issuing orders to one of his subordinates via an aide-de-camp. Speed comprised one of the key features of the emperor's strategic brilliance, and notwithstanding his lethargy at Waterloo he opened the campaign by seizing the initiative, crossing the River Sambre on 15 June with 125,000 men and advancing up the Charleroi Road en route for Brussels. On the following day his left wing under Ney met Wellington at Quatre Bras, while the emperor himself led the bulk of the army against Blücher at Ligny.*

bitter house-to-house fighting. Moreover, although Wellington could not spare troops to assist Blücher, by engaging Ney and the left wing he thus prevented their appearance at Ligny – though in truth he cannot be credited with deliberately seeking contact, since the initiative lay with the French. Thus, while the distraction created by Quatre Bras certainly did not compensate for Blücher's failure to maintain his own position, the Allies nonetheless remained intact, albeit still separated. But, crucially, the Prussians remained close at hand – at Wavre.

If Quatre Bras did not constitute the decisive victory which Napoleon desired, it did oblige Wellington to make a hasty retreat in order to protect Brussels. Similarly, although the Prussians suffered heavily at Ligny, they remained intact and retreated in sufficiently sound order to reorganise and fight another day. In this respect, while both battles of the 16th constituted tactical victories for the French, in fact, in light of the events played out just two days later, they may also be seen as strategic failures. On the other hand, Napoleon remained in the central position he sought and could still achieve his strategic aim, whereas on the 17th the Allies remained just beyond mutual support. Had the French either fixed Wellington at the crossroads or in any event pursued him with greater vigour than they did during the Anglo-Allied retreat of 16–17 June, they might have lengthened the distance between the two Allied armies – either scenario made all the more feasible when d'Erlon linked up again with Ney on the 17th, thereby strengthening his numbers. Similarly, Napoleon ought to have pressed home in pursuit of the Prussians, exploiting his victory at Ligny and denying Blücher the opportunity to recover from that serious blow. Instead, he was allowed to retreat north from Ligny towards Wavre, at the same time recalling Bülow's IV Corps and concentrating it with the other three. Napoleon, for his part, belatedly issued orders late on the morning of the 17th both to fix Wellington in place and to dispatch a corps of 30,000 men and ninety-six guns under Grouchy to stay in contact with the Prussians and prevent them from supporting Wellington.

*Napoleon on the eve of battle. His work habits went unmatched, with very long hours devoted to assiduous dispatch writing, the study of maps, considerable periods in the saddle surveying ground and attending to the minutest of matters connected with a campaign. That of 1815 demanded timely preparation, for whether or not Napoleon actually intended to renew his territorial conquests and restore at least a semblance of his lost empire, the Allies' determination to remove the emperor from power required him to assemble an army in great haste.*

Napoleon's late orders, combined with foul weather in the form of a torrential downpour, left his plans in tatters, for Wellington retreated north with sufficient speed not entirely to outpace his pursuers, but to enable him to disengage from them after a brief engagement in the morning, followed by a successful rearguard action which prevented the French from pinning Wellington in place. Instead, crucially, the duke withdrew to ground which, in marked contrast to that at Quatre Bras, he had studied previously and intended to occupy expressly for the purpose of making a stand. Similarly, with respect to the Prussians, by failing to outflank them at Ligny, Napoleon was unable to dictate the direction of their retreat, which common sense would suggest as east, toward Liège, thus tempting Blücher to continue along his lines of communication towards the Rhine and consequently away from Wellington.

Wellington's retreat north left his forces fatigued but still fully capable of engaging the French a second time. Moreover, the duke now knew the direction of Napoleon's main thrust and could deploy his forces accordingly for the next engagement. He also maintained contact with Blücher by courier, writing to him on the morning of the 17th, informing him of the new position he intended to take up and of his determination to give battle there if Blücher could offer a minimum of a single corps to assist him. Blücher replied at 6pm that he would do better than that: the duke could depend on the whole Prussian Army. Crucially, on receiving this message late on the night of the 17th, Wellington determined to fight rather than continue his withdrawal – a course which might have put a very different complexion on the remainder of the campaign. Reaching the area around Mont St Jean, he deployed his forces on a ridge just south of the village of that name. Napoleon followed up, positioning his forces immediately opposite the duke, minus the 30,000 men and 96 guns under Grouchy detached to follow and observe the Prussians, now camped in and around Wavre, 12 miles east of Mont St Jean.

An examination of the respective armies' strengths on the morning of 18 June may be instructive. With respect to the Prussians, Lieutenant General Thielmann's IV Corps of 25,000 men and 41 guns had not yet seen action, and by accounting for the severe losses suffered by I and II Corps at Ligny on the 16th – plus another 8,000–10,000 deserters lost to Blücher during the retreat from Ligny to Wavre on the 17th – one arrives at a total strength on the morning of the 18th of approximately 100,000 men and 283 guns. This reveals a staggering loss of 30,000 men in only three days – a third through desertion. Still, if Blücher were to remain true to his promise to assist his ally, this still represented a formidable force.

With respect to the French, accounting for losses of 17,500 men sustained on 15 and 16 June, particularly at the simultaneous

*Marshal Grouchy. A veteran of many campaigns of the 1790s, he was a distinguished cavalry officer in his early career and led divisions of the Grande Armée at Ulm (1805), Eylau and Friedland (1807), Wagram (1809) and Borodino (1812), where he was wounded. He also served in Spain, where as city governor of Madrid he put down the rebellion in May 1808. He led a cavalry corps in Russia and again showed his worth in the 1814 campaign in France. Like Ney, he defected from Bourbon service and joined Napoleon, fighting at Quatre Bras and then Wavre, where he performed an impressive fighting retreat.*

# A SMALL KILLING-GROUND

Amongst the many noteworthy features of the Waterloo battlefield are its narrow dimensions. Its full extent – the area in which troops were actually deployed though not necessarily engaged – measured only 5,500 yards (3.1 miles) wide from the western fringe of Merbe Braine to the eastern fringe of Frichermont, and only 4,400 yards (2.5 miles) deep from Rossomme in the south to Mont St Jean farm in the north. When, however, measuring the ground in which the actual fighting took place, the area forms an irregular rectangle which extends eastwards from Hougoumont, inclusive, a distance of approximately 3,800 yards (2.1 miles). Within these narrow confines at the opening of the battle, 150,000 men stood on the field, increasing by a third by the time all the Prussians who were to take part in the battle had arrived. All told, 200,000 men, 60,000 horses and over 500 guns were deployed in an area of a near-perfect square extending no more than 2.5 x 2.5 miles. In the ten hours between 11.30am and 9.30pm, 54,000 men fell as casualties – a rate of over 5,000 per hour – rendering the Waterloo battlefield more congested with fallen soldiers than any other patch of ground since, including the Somme in 1916. Around Hougoumont alone, an estimated 5,500 men became casualties in an area measuring 220 x 440 yards. Even this appalling statistic the horrific blood-letting at Plancenoit exceeded, with 11,000 killed and wounded choking the tiny village's houses, streets and churchyard.

engagements at Ligny and Quatre Bras, *l'Armée du Nord* on the 18th numbered around 105,500 men which, after deducting Grouchy's corps, left Napoleon 75,500 troops with which to confront Wellington. With perhaps 2,000 lightly wounded troops returning to the ranks from the actions of the 16th, one arrives at a slightly increased total on the field of Waterloo of 77,500 men – a figure slightly higher, but probably more accurate, than traditional estimates.

As for Wellington, accounting for the 17,000 troops and twenty-two guns he detached 5 miles to the west at Hal and Tubize to slow any wide French sweep round his right flank, he could dispose of 73,200 men along the 2-mile crescent-shaped ridge. This position had much to commend it, with the duke's left anchored on the villages of Papelotte and La Haie and his centre strongly bolstered by the farm of La Haie Sainte, which stood 275 yards in front of his main line, near the crossroads formed by the thoroughfares leading from Ohain and Charleroi to Brussels. On his centre-right and 450 yards forward of his main line, stood the formidable château of Hougoumont, a walled complex of farm buildings, chapel and adjacent orchard – ideal for improvised fortification and a superb advanced post. Appreciating the defensive capabilities of La Haie Sainte and Hougoumont, Wellington garrisoned them with some of his best infantry, thereby confronting the French with obstacles which they could not ignore, for any attack which sought to press past these positions would receive flanking fire from the defenders. Hougoumont in particular posed such a great impediment to a French attack, moreover, that its fall effectively stood as a prerequisite to any serious attempt by Napoleon to outflank the Anglo-Allied right.

Having chosen this ground in advance, Wellington had carefully studied its topography and considered its defence in the context of his years of experience in the Peninsula. The folds, dips and slopes around Mount St Jean stood to offer at least limited protection from French artillery, which invariably appeared in far greater numbers than his own (246 versus 157). He could also confidently expect to benefit from the previous night's downpour, for the sodden ground meant that round shot would simply plunge into the earth on first graze rather than bound along the field, causing havoc in the tightly packed ranks of allied infantry and cavalry.

The stage was therefore set for a colossal contest of arms.

# THE BATTLEFIELD:
## WHAT ACTUALLY HAPPENED?

Early phases: Furious French attacks on the Anglo-Allied right and centre.

**18 June 1815**

| | |
|---|---|
| **6am** | Bülow's IV Corps begins to move through Wavre in the direction of the Waterloo battlefield |
| **8.30–9am** | Anglo-Allied Army takes up final positions at Mont St Jean; Napoleon rides forward to La Belle Alliance to examine Wellington's position |
| **11.30am** | Battle begins with French attack on Hougoumont |
| **12.30–1.15pm** | British Guardsmen drive off French from the north side of Hougoumont and reinforce the garrison; at 1pm Napoleon's 'Grand Battery' of 80 guns opens fire |
| **1.15–2.15pm** | Napoleon receives intelligence from a Prussian prisoner at 1.15pm that Bülow's corps is *en route*; at 1.30pm main bombardment by Grand Battery ceases and d'Erlon's corps advances; Uxbridge orders the Household and Union Brigades to charge d'Erlon's corps; Prussian I Corps under Ziethen begins its march along a northern route in order to join Wellington's left flank |

**2.15–3pm**

18 June 1815

Anglo-German garrison continues to defend Hougoumont; Household Brigade fights French heavy cavalry west of La Haie Sainte and Union Brigade repulses d'Erlon's infantry; both Allied cavalry formations continue their charge into the Grand Battery and sabre the gunners, but suffer heavy losses from flank and frontal attacks by French cavalry; King's German Legion garrison continues to defend La Haie Sainte

## The Defence of Hougoumont and d'Erlon's Attack

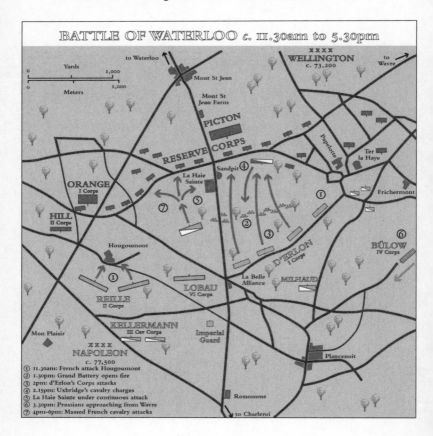

BATTLE OF WATERLOO c. 11.30am to 5.30pm

① 11.30am: French attack Hougoumont
② 1.30pm: Grand Battery opens fire
③ 2pm: d'Erlon's Corps attacks
④ 2.15pm: Uxbridge's cavalry charges
⑤ La Haie Sainte under continuous attack
⑥ 3.30pm: Prussians approaching from Wavre
⑦ 4pm–6pm: Massed French cavalry attacks

Action commenced at 11.30am when substantial elements of *Comte* Reille's II Corps (with a total strength of 20,200 men and 46 guns) attacked Hougoumont, whose capture the emperor regarded as vital, for it constituted the key to the Anglo-Allied right and centre-right. Without Hougoumont, the ridge upon which Wellington's infantry stood was considerably more vulnerable. By seizing it Napoleon also intended to draw off troops from other sectors of the Allied line, so depleting Wellington's strength elsewhere. Reille's attack constituted a diversion, but the French never intended an attack against it to be a major effort. Artillery opened up against Hougoumont while British artillery on the ridge replied. Inside, the garrison under Colonel Macdonell had loop-holed the walls, built firing steps and blocked the gates to the yard, apart from the main (north) gate which remained unobstructed for purposes of collecting supplies and maintaining communications. Hougoumont consisted of a series of buildings, cowsheds, barns and houses occupied by the gardener and farmer, with a stone chapel dividing two yards. To the east of the complex stood a formal garden surrounded by a 6ft wall, with an orchard immediately to the east. To the south, closest to the French, stood thick woods. In and immediately around this vital position Wellington posted a garrison of about 1,200 men – a combination of British Guardsmen, Hanoverians and Nassauers. It was a strong position, though the men were tired, wet and hungry from action at Quatre Bras and the retreat.

The advancing French reached the wood first, then the garden wall and the orchard, where masses of their infantry swarmed and surged. From windows and through loopholes the defenders fired while the wounded were carried or crawled into the barns, cowsheds and chapel. Rapidly the French made their way around the orchard and garden and reached the main (north) gate while it was still open. About thirty men and a single officer gained entry and engaged the Guardsmen in the courtyard in hand-to-hand combat while Macdonell and a handful of his men forced the gate closed. The intruders were eventually shot down or bayoneted, apart from a drummer boy whom the defenders left unharmed, while obstacles such as flagstones and farm carts were pushed against the gates to bolster the crossbar. From 11.30am until 1pm the fighting raged furiously around Hougoumont, the garrison clinging on desperately as masses of French infantry swirled round the walls, at times scaling them, only to be shot down or bayoneted in the act. French artillery continued to fire at and beyond the château, obliging British units on the slope behind to lie down to escape the storm of shot and shell.

Shortly before 1pm Ney learned that the Grand Battery of eighty guns he ordered established on rising ground near La Belle Alliance, about 700 yards from the Anglo-Allied ridge, was ready to fire, with 17,000 infantry arrayed in columns behind under d'Erlon and flanked by 800 heavy cavalry west of the Genappe road. Meanwhile, far on the French right, the first elements of the Prussian vanguard could be seen by Napoleon through his telescope on a knoll near the road at Rossomme. The emperor had only just completed a dispatch to Grouchy ordering him to continue pursuing the Prussians in the direction of Wavre, their last reported position. Changing circumstances now required an addendum: Grouchy was to detach himself and join the main body. In the event, the courier did not reach him until about 3.30pm, by which time it was impossible for Grouchy to disengage and march his corps, including guns and wagons, the distance required, over muddy ground, in time to make any more than a minimal impact on the fighting at Waterloo. In the meantime, the emperor shifted Lobau's corps to his right flank to forestall the Prussians once they reached the battlefield, though Napoleon's plan remained unaltered: a major assault against the Anglo-Allied line.

At 1.30pm the Grand Battery commenced firing; there was no precedent for such a bombardment in Wellington's long experience in Iberia. The 6lb and 12lb balls cut swathes through the infantry standing on the ridge before the onslaught. But while the bombardment constituted a dreadful ordeal for the infantry who had no choice but to endure it, it failed to break the men's

*Napoleon at Waterloo. While the emperor did take temporary shelter in a square of the Imperial Guard, this romantic portrayal of his role belies the reality that he spent virtually the entire battle on a small mound at Rossomme, out of view of most of the action and certainly beyond immediate danger.*

nerve and drive them off, not least because the duke had resorted to his old tactic of deploying many of his units on the reverse side of the ridge. Shots striking the top of the ridge continued on over and into the ranks of seemingly sheltered infantry, but many others passed completely over and often fell harmlessly into the soft earth, incapable of bounding further into units standing in reserve. Thus, part of the Allied front line – with one dreadfully exposed Dutch-Belgian brigade forming an exception – lay behind the comparative protection of the rear slope, where many colonels took the additional precaution of ordering their men to lay prone. This, in turn, left French observers situated beyond the valley which lay between the protagonists wrongly to surmise that the British had withdrawn under the heavy weight of fire, for concealed in the folds of the ground and shrouded in the smoke they seemed to those peering through their telescopes to have disappeared.

After half an hour the cannonade ceased and silence suddenly prevailed, soon broken by the distant sound of beating drums and troops shouting and cheering praise for the emperor. The valley now filled with a massive column of infantry flanked by cavalry and screened by clouds of skirmishers. This force proved irresistible to the light infantry arrayed in open order to oppose them, and the column, moving across open, undulating farmland, began to ascend the slope, passing on its right the orchard of La Haie Sainte and the small garrison lining its walls and occupying its buildings. Columns on this scale had succeeded regularly on battlefields before, particularly where a preliminary bombardment by massed guns had blown holes in the defender's front line, shattered the cohesion of his defence and crippled the morale of those awaiting the onslaught. But Napoleon's bombardment had not achieved this; d'Erlon's seemingly irresistible column faced steady, disciplined infantry – bloodied, certainly, by the cannonade but whose ranks remained firm. Moreover, columns composed of entire regiments advancing thus were not invulnerable, for apart from meeting the withering fire of a determined defender and slowed by thick mud and wet, shoulder-high rye, they presented a magnificent target to Anglo-Allied artillery and could not form square with the same rapidity as individual battalions. Impressive though the attackers appeared – marching as if on parade twenty-four ranks deep and about 150 men wide – thousands could neither see the object of their attack nor make use of their firearms, for only the front three ranks could issue fire. D'Erlon's corps might very well punch a hole through the defender's line, but if it failed, this unwieldy formation could not expect, under fire, to form into line to increase its firepower without suffering heavily in the process, especially if Wellington counterattacked.

As the column advanced British artillery fire rained down into its ranks, bowling over hundreds. Major General Bijlandt's Dutch-Belgian brigade, exposed on the slope, broke and ran over the crest of the slope, oblivious to the attempts of officers to restrain the men. When d'Erlon's column came within range of General

Picton's skirmishers on the front face of the slope, the defenders fired into the packed ranks advancing steadily towards them; but the fusillade failed to arrest the French, who closed ranks and continued their march to the sounds of 'Vive l'Empereur!' and the beat of the drum, believing the Allies to have fled their position. On approaching within 40 yards of a hedge the column halted, for an unwieldy column had no hope of traversing such an obstacle without hopelessly abandoning its neatly dressed ranks. It therefore stopped and formed into line, unaware that half of Picton's 5th Division had advanced and deployed behind hedges, from the cover of which they issued a devastating volley into the packed French ranks, only 500 of whom could answer with their muskets. No sooner had the Scots infantry discharged their weapons than Picton ordered them to charge, in the course of which a shot to the head killed him instantly.

The British line surged forward through the hedges, yelling, bayonets at the ready. A furious struggle took place with bayonet and musket butt, with the colour party of a British regiment fiercely contesting possession with a knot of French infantry determined to snatch some glory. Numbers might then have prevailed, but d'Erlon's unwieldy formation, surprised in the midst of deploying into line by an unexpected volley and bayonet charge by screaming British infantry, and unable to make the most of their firepower, began to waver, with the men of different units becoming hopelessly intermingled. Confusion reigned; men could neither find their officers nor officers their men, which in turn caused panic. In falling back the leading battalions drove into the ranks of those behind and soon men in their thousands made headlong down the slope for the safety of friendly lines.

## Charge of the Union and Household Brigades

Lord Uxbridge, commander of the Allied cavalry, was positioned on the right, near Hougoumont, when he saw d'Erlon's infantry advancing to the sound of the *pas de charge*. With no time to

## CAPTAIN ALEXANDER CLARK-KENNEDY CAPTURES AN EAGLE

While participating in the charge of the Union Brigade as part of the 1st (Royal) Dragoons he recorded the incident thus:

When I first saw it [the Eagle] it was perhaps about forty yards to my left and a little in my front. I gave the order to my Squadron, 'Right shoulders forward, attack the Colour,' leading direct on the point myself. On reaching it I ran my sword into the Officer's right side, a little above the hip joint. He was a little to my left side, and he fell to that side with the Eagle across my horse's head. I tried to catch it with my left hand, but could only touch the fringe of the flag, and it is probable that it would have fallen to the ground, had it not been prevented by the neck of Corporal Stiles' horse...

consult the duke, he ordered both the Union and Household brigades – seven regiments totalling 2,650 sabres – to charge. Into the midst of this chaos rode Sir William Ponsonby's Union Brigade consisting of three regiments – one Scottish, one Irish and one English, in all 1,332 men – situated about 300 yards behind the ridge. Eager to get to grips with the French, the brigade leapt over the hedge and through the ranks of Picton's Highlanders, knocking over some as they galloped ahead, with the Scots Greys shouting 'Scotland forever!' as they thundered down towards the fleeing French. Amongst these rode Sergeant Ewart, who cut down several soldiers in the colour party of the 45th *Ligne*, snatching away their regimental standard. The 1st (Royal) Dragoons performed the same feat, when Captain Clark-Kennedy seized the eagle of the 105th. The French stumbled in the mud and trampled grain, many cut down by the sabres of pursuing cavalry. Thousands threw down their weapons in token of surrender and were rounded up and herded away. But, like so often seen in the Peninsula, the cavalry officers, caught up in the exhilaration of the moment and incapable of reigning in the impetus of the attack, carried on up

*Lady Butler's stirring, late-Victorian depiction of one of the epic events of the battle – the charge of the Scots Greys.*

the slope and into the battery which had pounded the Allied line just prior to d'Erlon's attack. With ferocity the horsemen sabred the gunners and cut the traces and harnesses of the horse teams, losing Colonel Ponsonby somewhere along the way.

The Union Brigade did not charge alone. While it traversed over and through hedges, the Household Brigade, with their commander, Lord Uxbridge at the head of 1,319 sabres, advanced over the sunken lane which stood on the other side of the main road. Part of the brigade proceeded down the slope, skirting the west of La Haie Sainte and confronting about 800 cuirassiers who had accompanied d'Erlon's corps, while other squadrons charged in echelon over the crossroads and into the infantry, sweeping all before them. Yet with all control lost and the horses blown and deep behind enemy lines, any concerted attempt at reform and withdrawal became all but impossible. Uxbridge had shouted for the Scots Greys and Royal Horse Guards to cover the retirement of the other five regiments, but amidst the confusion, noise

## SERGEANT-MAJOR MARSHALL'S
### MULTIPLE WOUNDS

During the Union Brigade's charge against the Grand Battery, Troop Sergeant-Major Marshall of the 6th Dragoons received a sword cut which broke his bridle arm. He was then unhorsed by a lance thrust through his side, only to be cut several more times while trying to drag himself towards a riderless horse. After spending two days and three nights on the field suffering from a total of nineteen sabre and lance wounds he was discovered – and miraculously survived.

and smoke his shouts and the bugle calls ordering withdrawal went unheard. Sensing the moment opportune, 2,400 French cuirassiers and lancers now struck them in the left (eastern) flank and drove them off in confusion. Both formations sustained heavy losses – 632 casualties (48 per cent) in the Household Brigade and 616 (46 per cent) in the Union Brigade. Even before the survivors limped back to Allied lines their severely depleted ranks revealed that most of Wellington's cavalry could play no further role in the battle. True, they had blunted the attack of d'Erlon's corps – which represented a third of Napoleon's infantry and artillery on the field, and silenced the eighty guns of the Grand Battery – but even this remarkable achievement came at grievous cost to the duke's mounted arm.

Meanwhile, the rumble of the Grand Battery's cannonade had not gone unheard by Grouchy, 12 miles to the east at Wavre, where some of the marshal's staff urged him to march to the sound of the guns on grounds that the emperor had clearly made contact with Wellington and now required reinforcement. Grouchy, not yet having received revised orders, refused on grounds that his orders bade him pursue the Prussians; besides, he was at that time already engaged with Thielmann's III Corps. The Prussians, of course, heard the sound, too, and determined to fulfil his promise that he march to Wellington's assistance, Blücher was already *en route*, leading his troops through the morning and offering encouragement as his guns and wagons struggled through lanes – much more modest than the proper roads available to the British and French – made sodden by the previous night's torrential rain. The Prussians were unseen by both friend and foe at Waterloo, so when the vanguard came distantly into view around 1.30pm neither side were aware that this constituted only a fraction of the tens of thousands of Prussians on the march, some bound for Wellington's left, and others for the village of Plancenoit, on Napoleon's right flank, to the east of Rossomme. The bulk of Blücher's troops trudged slowly under difficult conditions but, all-importantly, unopposed.

*The charge of the Life Guards, the most senior mounted regiment in the British Army, dating back to the restoration of King Charles II in 1674. As a result of their assault against d'Erlon's corps, the Grand Battery and the counterattack launched by French cuirassiers and lancers, the Life Guards suffered severe losses: of the 490 officers and other ranks of the two regiments, 244 were killed or wounded, representing a staggering loss of 50 per cent.*

# THE PERILS OF ROUND SHOT

The Earl of Uxbridge, commander of the Allied cavalry, suffered a grievous wound from one of the last round shots fired by the French. Severing his leg, it proceeded over the neck of Wellington's horse. 'By God, sir, I've lost my leg,' Uxbridge is reputed to have said in a classic example of British understatement – if the story isn't apocryphal like so many quotations attributed to those present on the field that day. 'By God, sir, so you have', the duke replied in equally unflappable fashion.

*Prussian line infantry. These soldiers carried a standard issue musket similar to those of other armies but, perhaps unique to them, the Prussians carried no scabbard for the bayonet, thus requiring permanent fixture to the muzzle – a feature which reflected Blücher's doctrine that his men attack under virtually any circumstances.*

## Hougoumont and La Haie Sainte

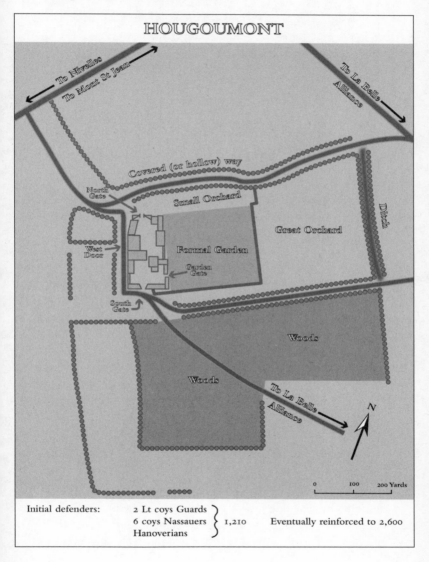

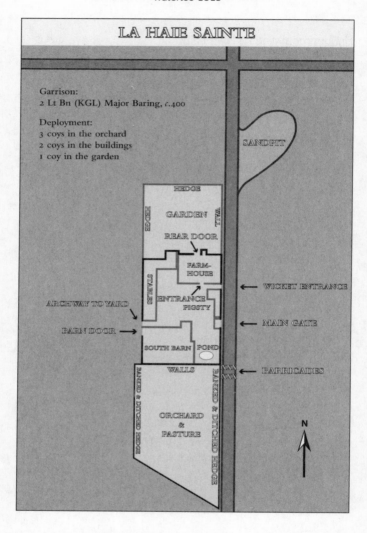

## LA HAIE SAINTE

Garrison:
2 Lt Bn (KGL) Major Baring, c.400

Deployment:
3 coys in the orchard
2 coys in the buildings
1 coy in the garden

SANDPIT

HEDGE

HEDGE

GARDEN

WALL

REAR DOOR

FARM-HOUSE

STABLES

ARCHWAY TO YARD

ENTRANCE

WICKET ENTRANCE

PIGSTY

BARN DOOR →

MAIN GATE

SOUTH BARN

POND

WALLS

BARRICADES

BANKED & DITCHED HEDGE

BANKED & DITCHED HEDGE

ORCHARD & PASTURE

N

In the wake of the destruction of d'Erlon's corps and the calamity suffered by Uxbridge's cavalry, a lull fell over the battle – apart from around Hougoumont, where Reille's infantry continued its vain and costly attempts to breach and scale the walls of the complex. Bruised and battered, both sides spent the period from about 2–3pm recovering and reorganising themselves. The artillery on both sides in the centre resumed their cannonade and, to the west black smoke swirled above Hougoumont, where the thatched roofs of the barn and outhouses had been set alight by howitzer fire. The flames soon spread to the château, causing dreadful suffering to the helpless wounded, who had crawled there for safety to join others left by their able-bodied comrades. These wretched men could not be evacuated by the few who remained to man the walls and defend the gates, leaving many to burn to death or succumb to billowing smoke. Paradoxically, the fires also contributed to the strength of the defence, for they barred the French from reaching the courtyard. By early afternoon the French had made their way around to the North Gate, but failed to batter this in and, most crucially, neglected to bring up artillery to breach the walls. When their attacks from this position receded, Macdonell summoned reinforcements and ammunition from the ridge. The defenders plugged or manned every gap and, miraculously, the place continued to hold.

As the fighting continued to rage in the early afternoon around Hougoumont, Wellington took advantage of the hiatus in fighting in the centre to return his infantry, many still lying prone as protection against the bombardment, to their sheltered positions on the ridge, thereby limiting the damage inflicted by the resumption of concentrated French artillery fire. Allied reinforcements arrived to the east of the crossroads, troops began to escort prisoners from d'Erlon's ill-fated attack in the direction of Brussels and some effort was made to collect the wounded and convey them to the village of Mont St Jean. Wellington, as had been customary in the Peninsula, rode along the ridge, calmly directing the re-positioning of units and offering encouraging words to his troops.

At the same time, Napoleon remained at Rossomme in an armchair. In his former days he, like Wellington, paid close attention to the conduct of battle, though on this day, suffering

## TRANSPORT FOR THE WOUNDED

The French developed the best method of evacuating the wounded from the field: the so-called flying ambulance invented by Baron Larrey, Napoleon's personal physician, whose horse-drawn vehicle was a light, well-sprung two-wheeled cart fitted with litters. The British, by contrast, possessed no special transport for the wounded.

from piles, the emperor preferred to devolve most of his power to his marshals and generals. Indeed, this was taken to an extreme; he remained *in situ* – a mile and a half from the principal points of action – and therefore unable to make the crucial decisions which must necessarily devolve upon the senior commander. When he did so, by dint of a galloping messenger, distance, the difficulty of the ground and fatigue necessarily led to delays in transmitting orders and the receiving of reports from subordinate commanders in the front line. As a result, most commanders sent him nothing, and the emperor himself only issued perhaps half a dozen orders between 11.30am and 5.30pm, a third of these of little significance. Actual command effectively devolved upon Marshal Ney who, though utterly brave in battle, constantly placed himself at the head of units in the front line, rendering him difficult to contact and detached from the wider perspective of the action – thus compromising his ability to act in the proper capacity of a commander-in-chief.

Having said this, during the lull in the fighting Ney could see the ridge line of Wellington's centre, but had no inkling of what lay beyond it. In the wake of d'Erlon's dreadfully failed attack, Ney received one of the few orders which Napoleon issued that day – to seize the farm of La Haie Sainte. The marshal duly sent for two brigades of infantry to attack it. The position was not ideally situated in Wellington's estimation, for it did not fit neatly into his defensive line – in fact it bisected it – and yet it could not go undefended owing to its proximity (200 yards) to the forward face of the ridge, which meant that its fall would split Wellington's army and enable the French to seize the vital Brussels road. Nor was it anything like as formidable an obstacle as Hougoumont. On the other hand, recognising this little farm's importance and determined to secure its preservation, Wellington had left within its walls a detachment of that most reliable body of troops, the King's German Legion. The farm itself was defended by approximately 400 men of the rifle-armed 2nd King's German Legion Light Battalion under Major Baring, with the brigade to which his command belonged, under Colonel Christian von Ompteda, occupying the area to the right of the crossroads, behind the farm.

La Haie Sainte consisted of a small farmhouse, barn, stables and other smaller structures and a pigsty, the whole surrounded by a stone wall, with access through the main gate facing east, and with an orchard on the south and garden to the north, both bordered by hedges. It stood along the main road running north–south with a sandpit, occupied by the 95th Rifles, at the northeast corner of the garden. The garrison had spent the night protecting themselves from the rain, but had received no orders to fortify the place in anticipation of attack. In fact, the engineers attached to them had been dispatched to help prepare the defence of Hougoumont. Thus, when it became obvious in the morning that battle was nigh, the garrison could do little more than place a makeshift barrier in the road near the main gate. Not only did Baring's men have no orders to prepare a defence of the place, they broke up farm carts for firewood, as well as the barn door which looked out into fields to the west. Having burned these, the men could not improvise firing platforms to enable them to see over the walls, thus leaving little else to do but to knock loopholes in the walls and place marksmen on the roofs. In the course of d'Erlon's attack, the small garrison had observed the French advance and even fired on it with their rifles, but little more could be done apart from watching cuirassiers and infantry swirl around the farm complex until driven off by Uxbridge's charge.

# THE ROLE OF ENGINEERS

These specialist troops served the critical function of building and repairing bridges, fortifying houses, clearing roads and conducting siege operations. They particularly proved their worth in the Peninsula, where Royal Engineers suffered losses of one-quarter through regular appearances in trenches and saps exposed to enemy fire and from leading the 'forlorn hope' – the lead element of infantry during an assault on a breach. In the British Army, the Corps of Royal Engineers consisted entirely of officers, only eleven of whom were present at Waterloo. This lamentable shortage of personnel goes far in explaining their absence from La Haie Sainte on the evening of 17–18 June, when Major Baring and his men worked feverishly to cobble together an *ad hoc* defence without any professional advice from those best suited for the task.

Then, at about 2pm, came the two brigades sent by Ney. One advanced straight up the main road while the other moved in oblique fashion across the fields. A cloud of skirmishers approached from the east, obliging Baring to summon all his forces into the buildings and yard, leaving the orchard and garden to the French. The defenders fired from loopholes, windows and rooftops while the French came so close to the walls as to seize some of the rifles through the loopholes. The attackers swarmed around the orchard and approached the wall of the barn, nearly penetrating into the courtyard through the archway between the barn and stable until the defender's fire shot down so many attackers that access became impossible with the whole area choked with bodies. Soon the barn caught fire, which the defenders, bearing kettles, managed to extinguish with water transferred from a small pond inside the compound. At about this time the attack dwindled away and the French beat a retreat. It had been a narrow escape, but in the process the garrison had lost many men to French musket fire and expended more than half their ammunition. Yet again, as with Hougoumont, the French had failed to employ combined arms tactics by bombarding the position with their heavy artillery, followed by a determined infantry assault designed to overwhelm the tiny garrison. Unless the French were prepared to change their tactics, Baring's position appeared unassailable so long as supplies of ammunition continued to reach him. With this in mind, he sent word up the ridge for more.

## Ney's Cavalry Assault

Developments in the afternoon: Ney's cavalry assault and Prussian approach.

| | | |
|---|---|---|
| 18 June 1815 | 3–4pm | Buildings in Hougoumont are set on fire; La Haie Sainte reinforced by three companies of King's German Legion infantry, but French make renewed assault on this position; remnants of d'Erlon's corps reassembles; gunner casualties from Grand Battery replaced and guns returned to action; at approximately 3.30pm the leading elements of Bülow's corps enter the Bois to Paris; at about 4pm Ney interprets movement towards the Anglo-Allied rear as a sign of general withdrawal and orders a major assault with his cavalry |
| | 4–5pm | Wellington's infantry under attack from cavalry form square; repeated French cavalry assaults fail amid heavy losses from Anglo-Allied guns and defending infantry; Lobau's VI Corps, encountering Prussians emerging from the Bois de Paris, are gradually pushed back to Plancenoit; French attacks continue against Hougoumont and La Haie Sainte |
| | 5–6pm | Notwithstanding the progressive introduction of reinforcements, French cavalry fail to break Anglo-Allied squares, though artillery inflicts some damage on Wellington's troops during periods of quiet between charges; by 5.30pm all of Prussian IV Corps is engaged against Lobau |

By 4pm the Prussians had not yet appeared in substantial numbers on the field and Wellington and his officers were growing increasingly anxious. On the other hand, the repulse of d'Erlon's corps had blunted the French effort in the centre and protected La Haie Sainte. Fighting continued to rage around Hougoumont, which became a major distraction for the French, who continued to funnel increasing numbers of infantry from other parts of the field in a struggle which, owing to its relative isolation from other events, amounted to a battle within a battle – an almost wholly separate engagement in which by continuing to preserve the integrity of the Allied centre-right, the relatively small number of defenders drew in French infantry needed elsewhere. On the other hand, in the centre, the Grand Battery, re-crewed by those who had survived Uxbridge's charge and supplemented by gunners and engineers drawn from elsewhere, continued to exact a heavy toll even to those positioned behind the slope, where hundreds died in the bombardment.

Then the guns fell silent, their sound replaced by the distant rumble of horses on the move. These advanced in their thousands, between the main road running past La Haie Sainte and the fields between it and Hougoumont – a distance of

## PROGRESSION OF A CAVALRY CHARGE

When ordered to attack, cavalry never launched straight into a gallop, but rather followed a prescribed sequence designed to enable the horses to gain gradual momentum without becoming exhausted before reaching the target. By starting with a walk, then the trot, gallop and lastly the charge, in theory cavalry could cover over a mile of flat ground before engaging the enemy, re-forming, and returning to friendly lines. The French and Prussians performed this sequence without difficulty, whereas British commanders frequently lost control of their units, prompting Wellington once to denounce cavalry commanders for 'galloping at everything'.

about a thousand yards. The phenomenon seemed perplexing to observers on the ridge, for the Anglo-Allied line, admittedly weakened by preparatory artillery fire and its infantry shaken, remained intact and ready to defend its ground, with its supporting guns continuing to fire, partly in a counter-battery role. An attack conducted by cavalry without supporting infantry of its own and – irrespective of numbers, launched against unbroken infantry – defied conventional wisdom. Indeed, Wellington initially believed the approaching wave of horsemen constituted some sort of feint to distract him from Napoleon's true intention: to execute a substantial outflanking manoeuvre well to the west of Hougoumont. Accordingly, the duke dispatched a cavalry brigade to investigate, and discovered the attack to be in earnest, directed against Anglo-Allied infantry which had yet to see any of the fighting, apart from the galling fire under which they had suffered now for several hours.

*Cuirassiers charge a square of Highlanders. Magnificent in terms of sheer spectacle, they knew infantry securely deployed in square remained impervious to their repeated efforts – yet carried on unswervingly. In short, Ney set this arm an impossible objective. Had sappers or gunners accompanied the cavalry's brave yet futile attacks, they could easily have dismounted and spiked Wellington's guns once overrun.*

The approximately 14,000 defenders watched with awe, incredulity and a strong measure of relief; for while all agreed the attack offered an imposing sight, the horsemen stood no chance against about twenty-five battalions of steady infantry with more than sufficient time to form mutually supporting squares. Moreover, the approaching cavalry obliged the harassing guns to cease fire, furnishing the hard-pressed infantry a much welcomed respite from fire to which the far less numerous and smaller calibre British guns could offer no equivalent reply. Thus, up came the cavalry in their thousands – mostly cuirassiers – but lancers and chasseurs, too, all led by the intrepid Ney, who had initiated the attack without consulting the emperor. Accordingly, the infantry lying down on the reverse slope of the ridge stood up, now shielded from the galling cannonade by the approaching tide of men and horses, and deployed into squares arrayed like a chequerboard, with orders to the gunners, positioned on the forward slope, to continue firing until the proximity of the attackers obliged them

*Cuirassiers at Waterloo. Their impressive equipment, uniform and accoutrements – especially the steel breast and back plate, maned and plumed helmet, and attractive horse furniture intentionally harkened back to the days of ancient Rome. Neo-classicism heavily influenced Napoleonic fashion and accounted for the presence of bronze eagles which adorned the standards carried by French units.*

to run for cover in the square nearest to hand. With no infantry in support of the attack, the gun crews could resume their posts once the squares repulsed their assailants.

No satisfactory explanation has yet come to light to explain Ney's decision for launching the cavalry in such numbers and without proper support, though many have speculated. He may have believed that Wellington was in the act of retreating, for like earlier in the day, just prior to d'Erlon's attack, Ney had observed the empty crest of the ridge and reached that conclusion – wrongly in the event. Some of his scouts may have managed to reach a point from which they could observe the other side of the ridge, there misinterpreting the movement of deserters to the rear or, more likely, mistaking for the duke's infantry the large body of prisoners being marched off towards the forest behind the Anglo-Allied rear. Whatever the cause, Ney called upon the whole of the heavy cavalry to follow him, including both Kellerman's and Milhaud's Reserve Cavalry Corps (6,700 all ranks and twenty-four guns). Unaccountably – for they answered only to the emperor's orders – the lancers and chasseurs of the Imperial Guard, posted near La Belle Alliance, a small farm located almost exactly in the centre of the French front line, followed suit, perhaps leading Ney to believe that Napoleon sanctioned the entire enterprise. All told, sometime after 5pm this onslaught amounted to nearly 9,000 magnificently accoutred cavalry: twenty regiments, representing just over 60 per cent of the French cavalry on the field. Whatever Ney's motive, the emperor, who continued to brood at Rossomme and had not observed this great spectacle, did not instigate the attack.

The cavalry cantered up the slope separating Hougoumont from La Haie Sainte – both of which remained under infantry attack – contracting their ranks to lessen the effects of small-arms fire on their flanks, but otherwise mounting the rise in magnificent splendour and incontestable bravery, with a frontage of perhaps 500 abreast and many ranks in depth. Allied gunners continued to fire at the advancing horsemen as quickly as they could before casting away rammers and slow matches and scurrying into the

*French lancer. Proper use of the lance required more specialised training than the sword, but once proficient a lancer could direct the point of his weapon with greater accuracy than his sword-armed counterpart. At Waterloo, lancers inflicted considerable damage on the Union Brigade by charging it in the flank.*

refuge of the nearest square. The sight of the sun's glint on the cavalry's helmets and cuirasses and the sound of the pounding of horses' hooves grew more palpable as the cavalry rode through the abandoned batteries and emerged over the lip of the ridge where the infantry lay ready, the front rank with one knee and the butt of the musket resting on the ground, while two further ranks stood behind, the whole forming a wedge of impenetrable bayonets – for a horse will not willingly charge headlong into such an obstacle.

On descending the other side of the slope, Ney and his followers now glimpsed defenders whose presence they did not expect to see, and with no hope of breaking the squares the flood of horsemen could do little more than lap around their edges, discharging their pistols and carbines – for apart from the lancers, they could not reach the defenders with sword or sabre.

The infantry, on the other hand, unleashed devastating volleys on successive waves of attackers whose formations

## PISTOLS

The flintlock pistol was largely the preserve of infantry and cavalry officers. The weapon, which required a smaller bore to prevent the ball from rolling out, was usually carried in a holster pointing down. Men in a colour party, that is, those responsible for defending a battalion or regimental flag, sometimes carried a brace of pistols like that of a naval boarding party. Notoriously inaccurate, the pistol was invariably discharged at point-blank range. Frustrated by the inability to break the infantry squares they encountered on the slopes between Hougoumont and La Haie Sainte, Ney's cavalry invariably fired their pistols at the steadfast infantry as virtually the only means of inflicting damage upon them.

broke up, forcing them to recede like an outgoing tide, leaving riderless horses careering about everywhere and growing mounds of wounded and dead on the ground, obstructing the progress of those waiting their chance to drive off Wellington's stalwart infantry. The attacks continued – sources disagree as to their number, but perhaps a dozen in all – with each departing wave met by gunners re-emerging from the squares to fire on the attackers' backs with canister and then, as the distance lengthened, round shot. But as the cavalry retreated, a fresh wave approached, repeating the futile and self-destructive process. Uxbridge committed the now-rested Life Guards, who performed well against their heavy cavalry counterparts, but the cuirassiers seemed always to return, first thundering up and, later, as the horses grew increasingly exhausted, slowing to little more than a walk, while in the intervals the French guns resumed their bombardment, inflicting grievous losses on infantry obliged to remain in their tightly packed, extremely vulnerable formations.

The defenders regularly dragged their wounded inside, unceremoniously cast the dead outside and closed ranks before the cavalry could discover a gap in which to ride through. Ensign Rees

*Henry William Paget, Earl of Uxbridge. During the Peninsular War he led Sir John Moore's cavalry at the end of 1808, achieving minor successes at Sahagun and Benavente prior to screening the British retreat to Corunna. He commanded the Anglo-Allied cavalry at Waterloo, where he had the peculiar misfortune of losing his leg to one of the last round shot fired by the French.*

## ABSENCE OF MEDICAL PAINKILLERS

Neither antiseptics nor anaesthetics existed at the time of Waterloo. Soldiers suffering from wounds to extremities normally underwent amputation before septicemia or gangrene set in. For chest or abdominal wounds the surgeons probed them to remove musket balls or shell fragments, but generally did so with unclean instruments, being ignorant of the risk of infection which this practice unfortunately encouraged. Thus, even if the patient survived the trauma of the surgical procedure – and stories abound of great fortitude under the knife – he often died of an infection whose cause surgeons could not yet deduce.

Gronow described the horrendous sight of the interior of a square that afternoon:

> Inside we were nearly suffocated by the smoke and smell from burnt cartridges. It was impossible to move a yard without treading upon a wounded comrade, or upon the bodies of the dead and the loud groans of the wounded and dying were most appalling.
>
> At four o'clock our square was a perfect hospital, being full of dead, dying and mutilated soldiers. The charges of the cavalry were in appearance very formidable, but in reality a great relief, as the artillery could no longer fire on us; the very earth shook under the enormous mass of men and horses...

All the while, Wellington rode amongst the squares, often taking refuge in them, steadying and encouraging men as the tide of horsemen ebbed and flowed, their departure replaced by renewed, exceptionally effective, artillery fire. At about 6pm, after nearly two hours of valiant though fruitless, wasteful sacrifice, the attacks subsided. The Allied centre, though badly mauled, stood weakened but not crippled, whereas the French had thrown away more than the flower of their mounted arm: they had squandered precious time – time during which the Prussians continued to filter gradually onto the field.

## CAVALRY VERSUS SQUARES

Instances of cavalry breaking squares are extremely rare – with only one recorded instance in the Peninsula; but if the infantry withheld their fire too long, discharging their muskets at perhaps 10m or less, a possibility existed that a wounded horse might plunge headlong into the hedge of bayonets, thereby inadvertently opening a gap in the square which the second rank of attackers might exploit.

## STATISTICS RELATING TO THE MASSED CAVALRY ATTACK, C.4PM

During the first phase of Ney's assault approximately twenty-two squares of Anglo-Allied infantry, totalling about 13–14,000 men, stood dotted along the Mont St Jean ridge, with about 8,000 cavalry to their rear. The defenders received supporting fire from eleven batteries, for a total of sixty-five guns and howitzers. The French initially launched ten regiments of cavalry, totalling about 4,400 men – mostly cuirassiers – which advanced along a compressed frontage of about 800m. These were supported by about seventy-six guns and howitzers – but such a large body of horsemen moving up an elevated position naturally obliged the crews to cease fire for a considerable period lest they strike their comrades, thus inadvertently relieving the pressure on Anglo-Allied infantry who dared not reform into column or line to render themselves less vulnerable to the frightful cannonade.

Therein lay, as revealed elsewhere on the battlefield, Napoleon's fundamental tactical error: his failure to launch coordinated, all-arms attacks. Had horse artillery accompanied the cavalry, not only might their gunners have spiked the Anglo-Allied guns, but they could have pounded their squares into oblivion, with the cavalry needed merely to complete their destruction by sabring those remnants still in a semblance of formation or, better still, to pursue the fugitives. Instead, after two hours' self-destructive carnage, the onslaught subsided, leaving the field strewn with weapons, equipment and ghastly ramparts of men and horses. Thousands writhed in agony on the ground while the infantry – exhausted and blackened with burnt powder – remained unmoved. Wellington's centre remained intact.

## The Fall of La Haie Sainte, the Struggle for Plancenoit and the Crisis in the Anglo-Allied Centre

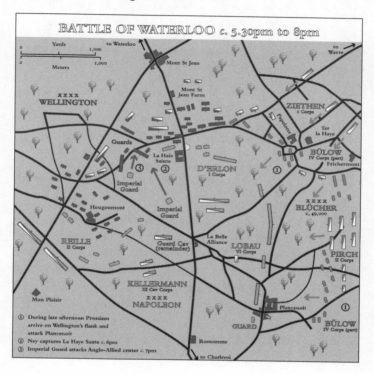

Evening phase: Fall of La Haie Sainte, Crisis in the Anglo-Allied Centre and Plancenoit.

18 June 1815

**6–6.30pm**      Fighting around Hougoumont continues, with the French controlling the woods and orchard but British and Nassauer garrison continuing to hold the buildings; at approximately 6.30pm the remnants of the garrison at La Haie Sainte, having exhausted their ammunition supply, abandons the position; Prussians take Plancenoit, obliging Napoleon to dispatch the Young Guard to retake it

**18 June 1815**

| 6.30–7.30pm | With the loss of La Haie Sainte the Anglo-Allied centre stands in mortal danger; French artillery continues to inflict heavy damage in this sector; Wellington begins to reinforce his centre with Dutch-Belgians and British cavalry; by around 6.45pm the Young Guard manages to retake Plancenoit, temporarily neutralising the threat to the French right and rear; Prussians then recapture the village, which two battalions of the Old Guard retake; leading brigade of Ziethen's I Corps links up with Wellington's eastern flank |
| 7.30–8.30pm | A false message that Grouchy has arrived is distributed along the French line to raise French morale; just after 7.30pm Napoleon launches eight battalions of the Imperial Guard against the Anglo-Allied centre, where heavy artillery fire inflicts serious losses on the attackers; fire from British infantry repulses the Imperial Guard; at about 8pm infantry from the Prussian II Corps begin assault on Plancenoit from which French are at last permanently driven out |
| 8.30–10pm | French rout begins around 8.30pm; Wellington signals a general advance; squares of the Old Guard retire slowly in fighting retreat; Prussians assume responsibility for pursuing the fleeing French; Blücher and Wellington meet south of La Belle Alliance |

By 5pm, despite dispatching four messengers up to the ridge to request ammunition, Major Baring had received none for his small garrison at La Haie Sainte. He did receive reinforcements (two companies of 1st Light Battalion King's German Legion, one company of 5th King's German Legion and one or two companies of Nassauers), so bringing his force up to about 550 strong by late afternoon, but powder and ball remained the priority. Around 6pm he sent desperate word that his position was untenable without further supplies. Unbeknownst to Baring, his battalion's ammunition wagon – containing, of course, the specialised

*Wellington and his staff at Waterloo. Casualty rates amongst the duke's staff and senior commanders were very high. Two of his staff were killed outright, one was mortally wounded, and three others suffered wounds but survived. Five generals were killed and ten were wounded. Of the twenty-five commanders of British infantry battalions, generally lieutenant colonels, one was killed and eleven were wounded. Three cavalry commanders died and seven were wounded out of sixteen.*

requirements for rifle-armed troops – had overturned on a road that morning and no one had bothered to recover its contents. Thus, the key position in Wellington's centre remained unsupplied throughout the whole day, its garrison having expended most of their ammunition not only by tending to their own defence but also in firing at the infantry and cavalry columns which had passed their position to engage the main line. The men were confident of holding the place so long as their ammunition held out, notwithstanding the fact that their casualty rate now exceeded 40 per cent.

Shortly after the cavalry attacks subsided, the Germans perceived the approach of a fresh advance against their position, both from the fields and along the road. Ney now renewed his previous attempt to seize the farm, based on the emperor's orders

## CALCULATING RATES OF SURVIVAL FOR THE WOUNDED

Of the approximately 57,000 casualties suffered at Waterloo, that is to say, dead and wounded, approximately two-thirds of these lay wounded on the field – or about 36,000 men once deductions are made for those whose severe injuries led to death on the 18th itself. Statistics available for patients who received treatment indicate that approximately 900 out of approximately 9,500 died once they reached a post offering medical attention, however basic. This mortality rate, about 9 per cent, compares very favourably with those of the First World War, fought a full century later – in which instances of death for evacuated wounded amounted to 8 per cent. This appears all the more impressive in light of the fact that the orderlies, drummers and ordinary soldiers who collected the wounded did not use stretchers, but rather laid a wounded man horizontally across muskets or carried him in a blanket supported by four to six men.

of earlier that afternoon. The French again swarmed along the walls, some penetrating the barn, where another fire broke out. Others forced their way through a door to the yard, only to be killed by thrusts of the bayonet. Still others tried to smash down the main gate with an axe, each successive attempt thwarted by men firing from atop the pigsty with what little ammunition they could still muster, much of it recovered from their dead and wounded comrades. But the attackers continued to come and when some climbed up on to the roof of the stables and began to fire into the yard against men now out of ammunition, Baring ordered the small remaining knot of defenders – wearied by hours of resistance and their faces blackened with burnt powder – to abandon the place, now a veritable charnel house. By this time only one route of escape remained: through the house and out the door to the garden. As the survivors made their way out, the

French finally managed to batter in the gate and poured into the yard in overwhelming numbers. In the event, of the approximately 800 defenders who had filtered in and out of La Haie Sainte during the course of the day, an estimated half had fallen in its defence.

The loss of La Haie Sainte seriously threatened the stability of Wellington's centre, not least because, fresh from their success in seizing the farmyard, the French followed up and engaged the King's German Legion brigade, situated 200 yards behind, from which Baring's men had been detached. The French proceeded to bring up all arms; skirmishers began to harass the main line from 80 yards' distance; artillery unlimbered within case shot range; and cuirassiers appeared in a dip to the right of the farm. The Anglo-Allies' vulnerability in this sector was now obvious, for Colonel Ompteda's Hanoverians, though sheltering in the protection of a sunken lane, had incurred heavy losses, with their ranks so thinned as to be unable to fill the wide gaps now plain for all to see. To the colonel's right stood a British brigade, but it too had suffered heavy losses and no reserves lay behind this inadequate front line. The Rifle Brigade, to Ompteda's left and across the main road, also stood behind the scarce protection offered by the broken hedges along the lane.

Seeking to maintain the momentum of the attack, the French drove forward towards Ompteda's formation, when the Prince of Orange dispatched one of his ADCs to the Hanoverian commander, ordering him to deploy one of his battalions in line and move against a line of skirmishers. Ompteda deemed this suicidal and, arguing that he held a sound, well-defended position, requested the order be rescinded on grounds that French cavalry, situated only 200 or 300 yards away, would simply run his infantry down before they could form square. Perceiving insolence, the prince appeared on the scene, accompanied by General von Alten, Ompteda's corps commander. Alten repeated the order, only to be queried by Ompteda, who asked for cavalry support and recommended an advance in square. The prince peremptorily identified the cavalry under cover as Dutch – clearly a mistake given their position behind the enemy front line. While the two Hanoverians persuaded the prince that the horsemen were clearly French, Orange nevertheless insisted that Ompteda obey his order. Accordingly, the battalion emerged from the sunken line, bayonets at the ready, and descended the slope in line formation, two ranks deep. The skirmishers duly withdrew into the cover of the hedges surrounding the garden of La Haie Sainte, and the cavalry – which in the event proved French cuirassiers – charged the advancing infantry in the flank, inflicting dreadful losses on Ompteda's men, their commander dying from a shot fired from the garden.

With the loss of an entire battalion the crisis in the Allied centre only deepened. A serious thrust by the French could now easily split Wellington's forces and oblige wholesale retreat. The duke, informed of the situation while riding on the extreme right, beyond the Nivelles road, ordered all the German troops and the guns that could be mustered to converge on the centre and close the gap. Some infantry, backed by the pitiful remnants of the Union and Household Brigades, were moved near the main road and formed

*French dragoon and dragoon sapper. Such men constituted medium cavalry – a designation placing them between the 'heavies' whose sole function was the charge, and light cavalry, who principally carried out reconnaissance and patrolling. Originally designed to fight on foot by riding into action and then dismounting, dragoons did not perform this function at Waterloo, firing their carbines at the halt and executing the charge, sometimes with cuirassiers.*

into square to block a possible breakthrough by French cavalry along that route. The duke soon appeared with Brunswickers to help fill the gap, all the while demanding that regimental officers hold their positions, for there were no reinforcements to hand and retreat was out of the question. The greatest crisis of the day was now upon him, for any substantial French attack could not be resisted. Salvation could come in one of two forms: darkness or the Prussians.

In fact, Blücher's troops were arriving, but not where Wellington desperately needed them, for the Prussian commander had directed them against Napoleon's right at the village of Plancenoit, a place not even visible from the Allied centre, with events there consequently unknown to the duke. Whether Plancenoit constituted a serious diversion or not Wellington could not determine; what he needed was several thousand fresh men to plug the gap in his centre created by the loss of La Haie Sainte or to strengthen his left, thereby freeing up troops there for deployment in the centre. Accordingly, one of the duke's ADCs galloped off and upon encountering the commander of the leading Prussian corps, Ziethen's, implored his assistance. Ziethen agreed, but would not engage the French without first assembling his whole corps, which still lay strung out along the line of march from Wavre. Meanwhile, one of Ziethen's staff officers went ahead to reconnoitre. Mistaking the large numbers of walking wounded, wagons, prisoners and deserters moving for the forest north of Wellington's line, he returned to his superior's side to announce the retreat of the Anglo-Allied Army, whereupon Ziethen declined to bolster Wellington's left and instead directed his troops south with the intention of linking up with the rest of Blücher's troops fighting at Plancenoit.

Plancenoit consisted of a small village of cobbled streets, walled gardens and stoutly-built houses. With the arrival from the east between 4.30pm and 5.30pm of Bülow's IV Corps, most of which fought savagely for possession of the place – and bolstered after dark by elements of Pirch's II Corps which in all committed 30,000

Prussians to its capture – the village became a cauldron of bitter, close-quarter fighting with bayonet, sword and clubbed musket. While the carnage initially involved Lobau's French IV Corps, as the weight of Prussian numbers began to tell Napoleon committed the whole of the Young Guard (eight battalions totalling 4,750 men) around 6.45pm, supplemented half an hour later by two battalions (1,163 men) of the Old Guard. Over the course of three hours the village changed hands several times, with mounds of bodies choking thoroughfares and, most grimly of all, the churchyard – leaving in the wake of this ghastly affair 6,350 Prussian and 4,500 French dead and dying amongst the ruins of this hitherto sleepy village.

## Napoleon's Final Gamble: The Attack of the Imperial Guard

Meanwhile, in the centre, Wellington's troops awaited the next French onslaught. Ney wished desperately to deliver it, but he simply had nothing left to commit. At last he held La Haie Sainte, but the garrison was not sufficiently strong – or fresh – to debouch (move into the open) and drive off the thin screen of Allied troops near the crossroads. His cavalry, weary and crestfallen at the horrendous losses they had suffered in the afternoon, amounted to a mere shadow of its former self, for the continuous, futile charges earlier in the day had left nothing but an *ad hoc* force composed of the remnants of the magnificent regiments squandered in the narrow gap between Hougoumont and La Haie Sainte.

But if Ney had no troops for a last, decisive thrust, Napoleon did. Since morning, eleven battalions of the Imperial Guard stood perfectly fresh and untouched at Rossomme. Sensing an opportunity, Ney dispatched an officer requesting permission to deploy part of the Guard. There was no time to waste, for only ninety minutes of sunlight remained. A breakthrough would spell incontestable defeat and clear the way to Brussels. However, the emperor rudely refused what he regarded as an impertinence. From his position, too far back from the main line and with the valley and ridge beyond it filled with the smoke of battle,

Napoleon could neither appreciate nor see the state of affairs, nor properly judge the soundness of Ney's request. The emperor consequently failed to appreciate the pivotal importance of the opportunity before him – and thus neglected to profit by it. By neglecting either personally to stay abreast of the day's events or to trust those closer to the action, Napoleon now missed the chance to achieve a decisive result while time still remained.

On the other hand, while Napoleon failed to understand that Ney held victory in his hands, Ney, in turn, could not appreciate why the emperor should refuse to release the Guard; that is, that the outcome of the bitter struggle for possession of Plancenoit remained in the balance – and that its fall would enable the Prussians to sever the main road of retreat back to France.

*Grenadiers of the Imperial Guard in barracks. Serving as Napoleon's bodyguard, they consisted of veterans of numerous campaigns and held a near-legendary, élite status. Until the severe manpower shortages experienced in the wake of the disastrous campaign of 1812 in Russia, the infantry of the Imperial Guard were rarely committed to battle. The fact that Napoleon detached many battalions of the Guard in an ultimately unsuccessful attempt to expel the Prussians from Plancenoit betrayed the increasing difficulties he was experiencing as the afternoon and evening wore on and his right flank grew more exposed.*

Their artillery was already almost within range of this route, a painful fact which opened the possibility of Blücher cutting the only line of communication and trapping the army on three sides, leaving it with no obvious route of retreat to the west. Of this potential catastrophe Ney stood totally ignorant. For this reason, Napoleon may perhaps be forgiven for retaining much of the Imperial Guard as the only remaining force capable of averting disaster. Perhaps an element of mistrust influenced his mind, as well, for if the marshal could send the cavalry to its destruction there was no accounting for what might befall the Guard in his care.

In the meantime, General Müffling, Blücher's representative at Wellington's headquarters, galloped after Ziethen and persuaded him to turn around and reinforce the duke's left. The Anglo-Allies, he insisted, were not leaving the field – but desperately required assistance. Ziethen agreed, and when his vanguard reached the Anglo-Allied left, British cavalry there began to move behind the ridge to take up a new post to the rear of the infantry still

*Marshal Ney during the retreat from Moscow in 1812. Ney's extreme heroism and the apparently genuine claim of his being the last men to cross the Niemen back on to friendly soil contributed to his iconic status and fully justified the impressive nickname, 'Bravest of the brave'.*

*A gunner of Prussian Foot Artillery (left) and Horse Artillery officer. The distinction between the two types of units lay in their relative speed. Foot artillery, like their horse counterparts, consisted of 6lb guns and 7lb howitzers in the light batteries, and 12lb guns and 10lb howitzers in the heavy batteries, whereas Horse Artillery invariably only employed lighter calibres – generally 6-pounders. More significantly, during periods of movement, the crews of foot batteries either walked or at best rode on the limber, while horse artillerists were mounted.*

standing fast in the centre. At the same time, word spread along Wellington's line: the Prussians were at last arriving in force.

Napoleon, by now situated at La Belle Alliance, observed the weakening resolve of the French near the crossroads; they could now see the Prussians approaching. Employing a cynical ruse, the emperor spread false reports that the approaching blue-coated infantry – difficult to distinguish at a distance from the similarly dressed French – were in fact Grouchy's. For a while his troops believed it – and word rapidly spread along the front all the way to Hougoumont, where it emboldened men still fighting to redouble their efforts against its stalwart defenders. With their energy and resolve flagging this news was precisely the boost the emperor's troops required. Meanwhile, as mentioned earlier, Napoleon sent two battalions of the Old Guard to retake Plancenoit, which they achieved, so neutralising for the moment the danger to the French flank and rear.

At 7.30pm, half an hour after Ney had requested the Guard, another lull came over the fighting in the centre – apart from continuous artillery fire. Then the silence was broken by the drum beat of a new attack against this sector of the Anglo-Allied line, now reinforced by the remaining ranks of units posted on the flanks. Napoleon had relented, sending forward five battalions of Guard infantry. By this time Ziethen's men had arrived on Wellington's left, but the emperor reckoned the opportunity to break the line had not yet passed. He placed himself at the head of the attack until, at the bottom of the valley separating the combatants he reached a quarry, where he and his staff remained behind as five of the eleven battalions of the Guard proceeded up the slope to the west of La Haie Sainte, where Ney assumed command.

Ney ought to have directed his attack up the road which led straight up the ridge past La Haie Sainte, for there Wellington's line stood at its weakest. Yet, unaccountably, he did not take that route. Instead, veering left after the quarry with the orchard of La Haie Sainte on his right, he proceeded through the fields between La Haie Sainte and Hougoumont, upon which lay the thousands of dead and dying horses and men of his earlier ill-fated mounted offensive. While it is unclear why he chose this line of attack, he may have wished to avoid contact with the newly arriving Prussians, now bolstering Wellington's left, and judged the Anglo-Allied right to be weaker. In any event, the quarry to the road measured 1,000 yards of open fields and offered a perfect killing ground for the batteries Wellington ordered to defend the area. Ground already sodden from the recent rain, churned up further by the great cavalry action in the afternoon, left the whole area a morass which slowed the Guards' advance. Moreover, the defenders – principally the brigades of generals Adam, Maitland and Halkett – though exhausted and badly mauled from the day's fighting, nevertheless still remained sequestered on the reverse slope, where the respite in fighting had furnished them a good two hours' rest.

In the course of the French advance, a round shot struck and killed Ney's horse – the fifth he had lost already since action commenced. With no available mount to hand, he proceeded on foot, sword in hand, while, as the columns drew closer, canister and case shot ripped through the serried ranks. Wellington's practice of constantly riding up and down the front line, shifting units and bringing in reinforcements as circumstances appeared to dictate continued to reap benefits, for he had foreseen the possibility of a final French offensive in the sector now threatened by Ney. With this in mind, he had re-deployed a number of batteries there and directed all infantry to lie down in the now trampled and bloodied rye, again offering them a degree of protection from French artillery fire. Having prepared the ground, the duke then positioned himself where he believed the brunt of the attack was to fall – behind two battalions of Maitland's 1st Foot Guards who, prone, could not see the advancing French, whereas the duke, mounted, could.

The five battalions of the Guard advanced steadily, and while their ranks suffered under the weight of artillery fire, they calmly closed them and continued seemingly unconcerned, sometimes momentarily disappearing in the thick smoke which shrouded the field or in the gently undulating ground. In support, three battalions of the Middle and Old Guard advanced but still remained beyond the valley southwest of La Haie Sainte, while another three stood in genuine reserve – one east of Hougoumont and the other two south of La Belle Alliance. The foremost attacking column, on reaching the top of the slope, appeared before the 1st Foot Guards while the other column approached slightly to the Guard's right. Light artillery advanced on the flanks, with a small body of cavalry in support near Hougoumont. The principal column detected no infantry before it – only the guns which continued to plough channels through its ranks – until it breasted the slope, just behind which Maitland's guardsmen still lay, awaiting Wellington's orders. Then, suddenly, perceiving the moment right, the duke cried out, 'Now Maitland! Now is your time!' He followed this, moments later with, 'Up Guards! Make ready! Fire!'. The crash of musketry at close range brought down hundreds of the attackers, some of whom halted and answered with uncoordinated fire of their own, while others, shaken by the sudden appearance of an enemy seemingly materialising out of

*The Imperial Guard, with General Cambronne at its head, defies calls for surrender from a British officer seen mounted on the left. Later in the century, with a revival of Napoleonic adulation – particularly after the rise of Napoleon III to power in 1852 – this episode played an important part in the efforts of sympathetic artists and writers to salvage something positive out of defeat, in this case by extolling the virtues of loyalty, heroism and self-sacrifice.*

## CAMBRONNE'S MESSAGE OF DEFIANCE

After the repulse of the Guard, General Cambronne accompanied the square of the second battalion of the 1st Chasseurs as it slowly withdrew under heavy fire towards La Belle Alliance. By the time he was called upon to surrender his unit numbered fewer than 200 men. Considerable controversy remains as to whether he replied in the romantic flourish often attributed to him: 'The Guard dies but does not surrender!' Wounded in the head by a musket ball and taken prisoner, he later denied the attribution. Others claimed he said nothing more than a defiant, '*Merde!*' Being a rough soldier who had risen through the ranks, in all probability he did issue the expletive – at least in the first instance.

thin air, began to waver in the ranks, evaporating the impetus of the attack. Before the assault could resume the Foot Guards launched a counterattack which, without achieving contact, drove their opponents down the ridge at the point of the bayonet.

Meanwhile, the left-hand column of the Imperial Guard met the 52nd Foot, under Sir John Colborne, which had marched in line over the crest of the ridge to meet the attack – not the column's front, but its flank. On receiving the 52nd's initial volley, the French halted and brought some of its files to face their assailants. At about this time, the 1st Foot Guards now fired into the head of the column, resulting in an intense exchange of musketry. Fired on from two sides by superior numbers, weakened by the carnage wreaked by Allied artillery during their slow approach, and staggering from the shock of finding their progress so unexpectedly opposed, the Imperial Guard broke and ran before reforming itself and marching once again to the ridge.

The repulse of the Imperial Guard sent shockwaves down the line of *l'Armée du Nord* all the way from Hougoumont on the left to Plancenoit on the right. The words '*La Garde recule!*' came as a thunderbolt: morale crumbled and panic ensued. Whether the

*To cries of 'Sauve qui peut!' – loosely translated as 'Every man for himself!'
– French troops take flight in undisciplined panic after the repulse of the
Imperial Guard. Relentlessly pursuing Prussian cavalry contributed greatly
to the high casualties already suffered in the battle itself and severely
narrowed the possibility that Napoleon could rally the army. Few battles
in history end in circumstances of such unmitigated disaster as Waterloo.*

sudden realisation that Grouchy's troops had not in fact appeared
on the field contributed to this frenetic atmosphere is unclear;
but the repulse of the much-vaunted Imperial Guard symbolised
nothing short of disaster, and to cries of *'Sauve qui peut!'* the
army dissolved into a fleeing mass, with most soldiers crowding
the road heading south past La Belle Alliance, while many others
– casting away their arms, the gunners cutting the traces of their
pieces – endeavoured to make the best retreat they could across
the open fields. Ten minutes later the duke removed his hat and
waved it, signalling a general advance intended to ensure that the
torrent of French troops did not somehow reform and establish
a makeshift defence. With the whole of the French Army in full
retreat, what cavalry remained fresh enough Wellington now
unleashed and ordered to pursue.

Those units of the Imperial Guard which Napoleon had not
committed to the fighting remained steadfastly deployed in square
on the road near La Belle Alliance while thousands streamed
past. The emperor took temporary shelter in one before fleeing

*Napoleon abandons his carriage and mounts his horse as the army dissolves around him, while elements of the Imperial Guard attempt to hold back the throng of fugitives. To the left, a gun team flees with a 6-pounder attached to its limber; in fact, the French abandoned practically the whole of their artillery on the field.*

the field. Bringing up artillery to point blank range, British officers called upon them to surrender. The roar of guns answered their refusal; hundreds were wounded and killed and the remainder taken prisoner. The pursuit continued into the night, conducted by the Prussians who, though fatigued from their march from Wavre, were eager to seal the fate of the French and left most of the work to their cavalry. Ziethen's men had been in action for little more than an hour and those in Plancenoit, which had changed hands several times that evening, had nothing left to offer. In short, badly mauled and exhausted, the Anglo-Allies were in no condition to pursue. The fugitives crowded through Genappe, a few miles south of La Belle Alliance, with Prussian cavalry at their heels, forcing the emperor to abandon his carriage, mount his horse and make his way to Paris with a small group of staff officers – but no recognisable body of troops.

# AFTER THE BATTLE

## The Butcher's Bill: Casualties

Waterloo cost all sides dearly – above all the French. Tabulating their casualties poses particular difficulties for historians, since it is impossible to distinguish between losses incurred on the battlefield and those suffered during the retreat following the action, some of which represent deserters rather than losses in killed, wounded and prisoners. At Waterloo Napoleon mustered 77,500 troops; rolls taken eight days after the battle reveal unit returns totalling 30,844 men, which represents an overall loss of 46,656, or 60 per cent of the army. The Prussians had already suffered heavy losses

## STAGGERING LOSSES

The 1st Battalion, 27th Foot (Inniskillings), numbering about 700 of all ranks, probably lost more men to French artillery fire than any other British unit at Waterloo: two officers killed and fourteen wounded out of nineteen, plus 463 other ranks as casualties, of whom 103 were killed and 360 wounded. Total losses amounted to a staggering 68 per cent of its strength – all suffered in the four hours after the unit arrived late on the battlefield at around 3.30pm.

*The wounded in the wake of battle. Those who found shelter in cottages
or barns like this proved the lucky ones. Untold thousands lay exposed
to rain and cold for as many as three nights before evacuation to field
hospitals or better equipped facilities in Brussels. In many cases, however,
the wounded succumbed to exposure, shock, blood loss or to murderous
swarms of looters – first soldiers and then the local peasantry – searching
for money, watches, medals and other valuables.*

even before Waterloo, about 30,000 men, a third of these through
desertion, in the three days prior to the 18th – mostly at Ligny.
At Waterloo the Prussians suffered approximately 7,000 casualties,
nearly 90 per cent of these lost to Bülow's IV Corps during the
carnage around Plancenoit. The Anglo-Allies suffered casualties of
17,000, or nearly a quarter of those engaged.

## Factors Contributing to Victory and Defeat

French errors connected with the Waterloo campaign in general,
as well as with the battle in particular, abound; thus, the Allies'
success must not be attributed solely to decisions of their own
making, but rather in combination with an analysis of French
actions – and Allied errors.

Napoleon committed a fundamental error in failing to initiate his attack until 11.30am. He over-confidently assumed that Grouchy possessed the manpower and skill to occupy the whole of the Prussian Army at Wavre, keeping the Allies apart long enough to inflict a crippling blow on Wellington before reinforcements could arrive from the east. Time was of the essence: by attacking at first light Napoleon would have gained for himself several more hours in which to confront the Anglo-Allies without Prussian assistance. Instead, by waiting until nearly midday in the hopeless expectation that the ground would harden sufficiently to increase the efficiency of his artillery, the emperor cast aside the chance to fight Wellington on his own, with virtual parity in numbers – albeit the French still facing a well-positioned defender.

Indeed, in light of the strong position he encountered at Waterloo, Napoleon might have pursued an altogether different course of action, such as withdrawing and fighting another day, possibly on a field of his own choosing or in any event one not of Wellington's. Alternatively, the emperor might have executed a wide outflanking manoeuvre, thereby denying the Anglo-Allies the advantages offered to them from the possession of Hougoumont and La Haie Sainte. To his cost, Napoleon chose an unimaginative frontal assault against Wellington's main line in a desperate bid to split his army in two, seize control of the critical Brussels road and march on the capital and Antwerp, thereby severing Wellington's lines of supply and communications across the Channel. Thus, while Napoleon chose the correct strategic objective, the tactics he employed to achieve it were fatally flawed.

Some have criticised the duke for detaching such a large formation, 17,000 men and 22 guns – representing 23 per cent of his force – to the area around Tubize and Hal, for the sake of protecting his extreme right from, as it happened, an attack which never transpired. Once Wellington became aware that Napoleon did not intend to undertake a wide encircling movement no time remained to recall the detachment to participate at Waterloo. Yet Wellington could not have known that the French would execute

*Napoleon at Waterloo. The campaign is replete with 'what ifs?' What if the emperor had succeeded in separating the Allied armies sufficiently to deny them mutual support? What if Blücher had been captured at Ligny after falling from his horse? What if Grouchy had marched to the sound of the guns? But perhaps the greatest question of all: what if Napoleon's health had permitted him properly to command at Waterloo instead of Ney?*

a full-frontal attack rather than attempt to proceed on Brussels via Mons over what amounted to a more circuitous yet much less encumbered route. As Napoleon was known for his great flanking manoeuvres and Wellington had not fought him personally before, detaching men from Lord Hill's II Corps appears to have been a sensible decision under the circumstances.

One may argue with considerable merit that Napoleon should never have attempted to eject the Anglo-Allies from the Mont St Jean ridge – at least not by the methods he employed. Both Hougoumont and La Haie Sainte sat forward of Wellington's main position, offering excellent anchoring for his line; folds in the ground also concealed much of the duke's position from French view, including the important laterally positioned Ohain road which stretched east–west, thereby allowing easy communication and supply to units along most of the front line. The topography

*Lieutenant General Rowland, Lord Hill, a very successful veteran of the Peninsular War and commander at Waterloo of the Anglo-Allied II Corps, a force which after detaching 17,000 men to watch Wellington's extreme right at Hal numbered about 10,000 men. Hill's particularly hard-hit formation held firm throughout the day, so contributing to the iconic status of a battle in which steadfastness and grim endurance epitomised the conduct of the Anglo-Allied Army.*

and the physical obstacles which accentuated these advantages entirely suited the temperament and experience of British troops, who had fought numerous actions in the Peninsula on the basis of Wellington's carefully considered choice of ground.

On a more strategic level, although Napoleon's rapid advance into Belgium on 15 June caught the Allies by surprise, he might well have succeeded in maintaining his authority simply by consolidating his power within France, depending on the frontier forts to slow his enemies' advance before engaging them on home soil, by which time the combined numbers of French forces would have reached several hundred thousand. After all, with far fewer numbers available to him in 1814, Napoleon had performed a series of miracles until finally overwhelmed.

Still, having rejected that option and proceeded with his campaign in Belgium, the emperor failed to order Ney to take the crossroads at Quatre Bras until too late in the day, rendering it impossible for him – especially without d'Erlon's assistance – to inflict a properly decisive blow upon Wellington. D'Erlon himself cannot be blamed for marching his corps for six hours on the 16th – in the course of which he failed to arrive at either battlefield – for he possessed contradictory and confusing orders from Ney, Napoleon and Marshal Soult, the Chief of Staff. One might well argue that, appreciating that he could not fight at both Quatre Bras and Ligny, and that time would be uselessly spent on the march given the distances to cover, d'Erlon ought to have made an independent decision; that is, to obey one order at the expense of another, and simply intervene where he reckoned he could achieve the most good. But that is to assign to a commander rather more initiative than that to which he was entitled. The same principle may be applied to Grouchy, some of whose staff begged him to march west to participate in what appeared to be a much larger engagement than that into which he became simultaneously embroiled at Wavre with only 25,000 Prussians – a mere quarter of Blücher's force.

Much might also have been accomplished on the 17th, for with both Wellington and Blücher forced to retreat – the Prussians in particular – Napoleon failed to grasp the opportunity to pursue them with greater vigour, so placing himself in a position to engage them once again and inflict a mortal blow, or at least channel the direction of their retreat so as to eliminate the opportunity of their co-operating further. By permitting Wellington to withdraw from Quatre Bras, the French enabled the duke to establish himself in a pre-arranged position of considerable strength. In the case of the Prussians, although badly mauled, they extricated themselves entirely from Ligny, moving northwards to Wavre, unmolested.

Whether Napoleon ought to have detached Grouchy at all is debatable. On balance, a covering force of some kind appears sensible, even if only to delay any Prussian attempt to link up with Wellington at some subsequent engagement. But having made the decision to send Grouchy, the marshal required timely orders – which Napoleon ought to have issued early on the 17th and not in the afternoon – for after midday Blücher's exact whereabouts were unknown. In the event, Grouchy of course *did* engage the Prussians; specifically, III Corps and elements of the other three. Yet the distribution of Prussian troops enabled nearly all of them to avoid being pinned – and the rest is history. Retaining Grouchy with the main body might have offered some advantages, of course, such as an adherence to the fundamental precept of maintaining concentration of force; yet retaining Grouchy with the main body might simply have enabled all four of Blücher's corps to arrive at Waterloo all the more rapidly.

In judging Grouchy's decision not to march to the sound of the guns immediately upon hearing the roar of the Grand Battery, one must not profit unfairly from the benefit of hindsight. To have left his position at Wavre would have constituted the defiance of orders received as recently as 10am that day. Even had he marched for Plancenoit, where in the event the impact of Prussian intervention at Waterloo was greatest, he is unlikely to have reached the village in time to offer support to its beleaguered defenders, for the corps of Pirch and Thielmann probably would have interposed themselves between his line of march and the village, thus enabling Ziethen and Bülow to proceed towards Wellington's left and down to Plancenoit unmolested. Over this whole debate Grouchy is far less to blame than his emperor, for the stark fact remains that – in light of the serious defeat he had inflicted on Blücher two days earlier – Napoleon simply did not believe the Prussians capable of so rapid a recovery, and therefore failed to anticipate any meaningful Prussian intervention on the 18th.

This miscalculation, in turn, strongly contributed to Napoleon's failure to appreciate that time stood clearly against him. With the protection of his right flank uncertain owing to ignorance of Blücher's dispositions and intentions, Napoleon ought to have appreciated the vital importance of launching his attack against Wellington as soon as the preliminary bombardment of Anglo-Allied lines could be construed as sufficient to support d'Erlon's offensive. Any sensible commander could appreciate the benefits to be accrued to the deployment of artillery on dry ground; but to wait until 11.30am – well after sunrise – to fire his guns proved utter folly. No prospect of serious sunshine existed for the 18th, and in light of the torrential downpour of the previous evening, the emperor could not realistically hope for much firmer ground by midday. Considerable blame for delay must also rest on the shoulders of the Chief of Staff, Soult, who failed to concentrate and deploy forces early enough on the morning of the battle.

Napoleon badly fixed his own headquarters. He had briefly moved his post from Rossomme to another mound, close to La Belle Alliance, but not for any substantial period. The latter position would have furnished him with a commanding view of the valley separating the two armies akin to Wellington's on the slope opposite. The emperor did not need to be in the thick of things at the front line; rather, circumstances demanded he place himself in a position personally to observe the progress of the fighting and to maintain direct control of affairs. By remaining aloof he left matters entirely in the hands of Ney, who in turn failed to step back from the action and view it with the wide perspective required of a senior commander. Conversely, Wellington continuously rode along

*Wellington and Blücher meet at La Belle Alliance in the aftermath of the fighting. The Prussian commander proposed that the battle assume the name of this place, but the duke chose 'Waterloo' owing to its ease of pronunciation, notwithstanding the fact that no fighting took place in the village of that name, which lay just north of Mont St Jean.*

the front, monitoring events, offering words of encouragement, ordering up reinforcements and deploying troops as needed.

Napoleon's position on the battlefield may appear less relevant in light of the fact that he served merely as the *de jure* commander, with Ney actually in charge. Suffering from piles and physically and psychologically disengaged from the battle until late in the afternoon, the emperor was unable properly to observe the fighting and relied on messengers to apprise him of events. Thus, one sees the paradox of Ney positioning himself too close to the action – sometimes personally leading attacks – while, conversely, Napoleon stood too far from it. The two commanders were not in touch between 9am and 7pm, thus producing a vacuum in command, whereas Wellington, as discussed, adopted the correct procedure – riding across the slopes of Mont St Jean surveying the action and making decisions based on personal observation. Neither Ney nor Napoleon occupied the equally advantageous positions on the opposite ridge, from which they ought to have issued orders, received reports and generally made themselves regularly accessible to subordinates.

Napoleon's failure to establish the Grand Battery earlier represented one of at least two errors connected with the French deployment of artillery at Waterloo. Formidable though it was and almost impervious to unsupported infantry, neither Hougoumont's gates nor walls could have withstood artillery fire deliberately sighted to batter them down – especially the western side of the château and farm, which the wood did not mask as it partially did the south gate. The French also made little attempt to set fire to the complex – particularly its vulnerable roofs – by employing howitzer fire, with or without heated shot. Similarly, the French failed to direct artillery fire against the walls of La Haie Sainte; and yet the Grand Battery stood only 300 yards away. With a breach made, Napoleon possessed plenty of infantry to overwhelm the garrison, whereas the position did not fall until evening – and only as a consequence of poor supply. In short, judicious deployment of artillery would have reduced the place to a shambles. In truth, it was a miracle the farm did not fall sooner, for no one answered Baring's repeated pleas for ammunition, either as a result of incompetence or the fact that no one bothered to rescue the overturned wagon which contained the ammunition and powder peculiar to the Baker rifles carried by his men. If Wellington surely cannot be blamed for this, he must answer for his failure to dispatch engineers to fortify the place the night before the battle.

Not merely by failing to employ artillery correctly – but by allowing their infantry to be sucked into an unforeseen quagmire – the French ensured that the fight for Hougoumont would

*Wellington at Waterloo. Despite his victory there, he bungled three days before by failing to act rapidly to news of the French capture of Charleroi, which enabled Napoleon to maintain the initiative and strike with advantage at Quatre Bras and Ligny the following day. The duke's hesitation also placed Blücher in an awkward position, for having promised on 3 June to move Anglo-Allied troops closer to the Prussians in the event Napoleon attacked, Wellington failed to do so on the 15th.*

continue practically unabated for eight hours, draining away brigade after brigade from other sectors of the battlefield to no purpose. Specifically, through this form of unintended escalation the fight absorbed two out of three of Reille's divisions in a desperate struggle which cost him something on the order of 4,000 casualties, or practically a third of those committed to the assaults launched against the farm's formidable buildings, wood and orchard.

The methods adopted to assail Hougoumont and La Haie Sainte revealed an abject failure to employ combined arms (in this case infantry and artillery), thus contributing significantly to ultimate French defeat at Waterloo. The same principle applied to Ney's uncoordinated cavalry charges, which required (at least some) infantry and (more) artillery support. There is no question that Ney sacrificed the reserve cavalry to no purpose, squandering some of the best horsemen in Europe in a series of futile attacks. Not only did the assaults proceed largely unaccompanied by horse artillery, the presence of so many horsemen confined to a relatively small area offered a splendid target to Allied artillery, but also actually afforded a respite from French artillery fire to the defenders. Ney also ill-timed his assault, for by 4pm, in the absence of sufficient firepower deployed against them over the course of the previous four and a half hours, Wellington's approximately twenty-five squares – perhaps as many as 14,000 men – remained fully capable of repelling cavalry, irrespective of their number, especially when one takes into account the standard military maxim that to stand a reasonable chance of success an attacking force must enjoy at least a 3:1 superiority. This already serious disparity grew all the worse since, as Ney's cavalry mounted the ridge unsupported by infantry and artillery, Wellington's guns continued to fire to the very last moment, bolstering his infantry's confidence.

*The Household Brigade gallops past Wellington. Commanded by Major General Lord Edward Somerset, this élite formation consisted exclusively of Guards heavy cavalry, but with a field strength of only 1,319 officers and men mustered little more than half its proper establishment. Together with the Union Brigade it first charged d'Erlon's advancing corps, then proceeded to overrun the Grand Battery before French cavalry counterattacked and drove it off in disarray, with half its strength hors de combat (unable to fight).*

In short, if the cavalry was to be unleashed against the Allied line, Ney executed his attack too early – and then waited too long to disengage – a classic case of 'reinforcing failure'.

Still, this is not to ignore the misuse of Allied cavalry, for Uxbridge disastrously overextended himself once both brigades had overrun the French guns; and yet, given Wellington's defensive position, his determination to hold his ground rather than counterattack, and the facility with which his cavalry repulsed Napoleon's principal infantry assault of the day, he could afford substantial losses to his mounted arm more readily than his opponent.

In the evening, with the Prussians debouching from Plancenoit, Napoleon had no choice but to commit the Guard; but whether or not he should have sent them forward when La Haie Sainte fell – and thus exploited in a timely fashion the

*Napoleon at Waterloo. Upon returning to French soil Napoleon immediately turned to the task of creating an army, which he accomplished with the same remarkable speed and efficiency which had characterised his previous years as emperor. In so doing he literally stole a march on Allied forces in Belgium which were initially widely dispersed. At the same time, Parliament in London voted to resist his restoration while the Allied heads of Europe declared Napoleon an outlaw and pledged to destroy him.*

moment when Wellington's line appeared most vulnerable –
remains contentious. Napoleon should have attacked at 7pm;
instead, he waited until 7.30pm – a vital thirty minutes in which,
although his troops retook Plancenoit, he lost the opportunity to
break the Anglo-Allied centre. The emperor rightly appreciated
that he must retain part of the Guard in his centre while sensibly
detaching a portion to hold or retake Plancenoit; but to wait
until after the critical moment had passed – after his forces still
retained the ability to split the Anglo-Allied centre – must figure
in the long tally of missed French opportunities at Waterloo.
Moreover, when they proceeded with an attack – led by Ney
rather than Napoleon – the Imperial Guard ought to have gone
straight up the main road past La Haie Sainte, not in the open
fields between that farm and Hougoumont, where concentrated
artillery fire swept over 1,000 yards of open ground.

Despite this catalogue of errors – mostly on the French side but
by no means confined to it – the outcome of Waterloo must not
be viewed as a foregone conclusion. After all, Wellington himself
famously described the action as 'A close-run thing'. The French
enjoyed high morale, for Napoleon represented in his troops'
eyes a man of immense military prestige whose reputation for
succeeding against the odds strongly boosted their spirits on
the 18th, only two days since defeating the Allies at separate
engagements. The French well out-gunned Wellington and, in
sharp contrast to the Anglo-Allies, they were distinguished by their
homogeneity, with quality consistent across all units, requiring no
recourse to the process of intermingling foreign with French units
to ensure a leavening between them.

One may argue with some justice that, as previously
explained, since commonly held doctrine advises a 3:1 numerical
superiority to the attacker in order to compensate for the innate
advantages accruing to a defender, Napoleon ought to have
declined battle at Waterloo in the first place. The French barely
outnumbered their opponents – by a few thousand, not enough
to offer any genuine benefit, particularly in light of Wellington's

*Napoleon amongst his troops, whose tactical proficiency in the past had provided their charismatic commander with success in a long series of brilliant campaigns, particularly in the years 1805–07.*

strong position. The French held the advantage in cavalry – about 3,000 more than Wellington – and, above all, in artillery, with 246 to 157 guns, a difference of eighty-nine; but as has been shown, the French misused both arms, thus squandering their advantage in numbers. A detailed comparison of the numbers deployed reveals remarkable parallels:

|  | Wellington | Napoleon |
|---|---|---|
| Infantry | 53,850 | 53,400 |
| Cavalry | 13,350 | 15,600 |
| Artillery | 157 guns+rockets | 246 guns |

Such figures highlight the relative importance of the Prussian presence on the field towards the end of the day's fighting, even though the Anglo-Allies had done much of the work by the time the 31,000 men of Bülow's IV Corps had begun to make a genuine impact between 4.30pm and 5.30pm. By as early as

1.30pm, aware of their approach and concerned by the threat they posed to his right, Napoleon ordered Lobau's VI Corps, consisting of 10,600 men, to defend his right flank. By doing so, the emperor denied himself their use against Wellington. Therefore, in re-tabulating the numbers available to prosecute an attack, the French actually deployed fewer troops than the Anglo-Allies, with 66,900 against 73,200. Bare numbers alone do not, of course, account for success or failure, since a myriad of other factors inevitably influence conditions, such as training, tactics, leadership, morale and other considerations. Yet given the British soldier's reputation for doggedness and his remarkable ability to defend from cover, the French might have been well advised to seek an alternative to a simple frontal attack.

What assessment, finally, can be made of the impact of the Prussians' arrival; which is to say, could Wellington have won the battle without their assistance? The problem of determining the extent and impact of Prussian influence on the outcome of the battle remains highly contentious but not insoluble. Any reasonable conclusion must rest on an examination of numbers and timings. Total Prussian forces actually participating at Waterloo numbered approximately 49,000 men and 134 guns. Only one corps, Bülow's, with 31,000 men and eighty-six guns, reached the battlefield with all its troops and artillery as a single cohesive force, though its leading elements did not arrive until around 4.30pm, with the remainder on the field within approximately an hour. About 12,800 men from Pirch's II Corps arrived between 6.30pm and 7.30pm and something on the order of 5,000 troops of Ziethen's I Corps joined the fighting between about 7.30pm and 8.00pm. These troops, in drawing off Lobau's entire corps plus elements of the Imperial Guard dispatched to protect the emperor's right, specifically in around Plancenoit, clearly denied Napoleon the use of these forces against Wellington, and there is no telling what impact their judicious employment might have served against the Anglo-Allies, particularly after the fall of La Haie Sainte – provided, of course, that such troops still remained available after 6.30pm.

Yet in light of the whole series of French tactical errors committed throughout the course of the day, there is no reason to believe that, even had the whole of Blücher's forces remained at Wavre on the 18th, Napoleon could drive Wellington from his position. With approximately equal numbers on both sides; with the duke holding the advantage which, all other factors being equal always accrues to the defender; with no attempts by the French to outflank the Anglo-Allied position; with no ability of Napoleon at least to even, if not better, the odds by exploiting the element of surprise; and, perhaps above all, in light of the wasteful errors committed by the French in assailing Hougoumont and the Anglo-Allied centre without proper use of combined arms tactics, it is only reasonable to conclude that Wellington stood every chance of succeeding against Napoleon – even without Prussian assistance.

# THE LEGACY

## Political and Strategic Consequences

Quite apart from lives lost and bodies maimed, Waterloo cost Napoleon, and France as a whole, dear – politically, economically and strategically. Internally, with the Bourbons restored for a second time, the French people faced a greater reversal of revolutionary reforms than in the previous year. Many Napoleonic officers were hunted down in the 'White Terror' and the mood of the nation clearly shifted, as reflected in the election of August 1815, whereby the great majority of the electorate – albeit not one chosen on anything like a democratic basis – overwhelmingly rejected liberal principles and the military clique so closely associated with Napoleonic rule. The extent of this rejection may be appreciated by the fact that in November the Chamber of Peers, by a vote of 157 to 1, condemned and executed Ney on the perfectly reasonable charge of treason. This decision only confirmed the prevailing view across France that whatever the past sins of the monarchy, a curtain surely now had finally to be drawn across the days of empire and the principle of *la Gloire* – the pursuit of glory through force of arms. Nor did peers merely constitute Bourbon appointees; many had come to power under the empire, most drawn from the untitled, albeit comfortable

*Marshal Ney. Not alone amongst contemporaries of the French Army who revelled at being in the thick of things, irrespective of the risks involved, Ney was a fiery, red-headed Gascon, who suffered no fools and expected the highest standards of discipline from his troops. Few men stood higher in their estimation than the intrepid Ney, whose life ended in front of a Royalist firing squad for his desertion to Napoleon's cause.*

classes, and though doubtless inclined to curry favour with the new regime in order to maintain their respective positions in society, were not unduly prevailed upon to seal the marshal's fate. In short, Ney's death reflected a fundamental change of political attitude in France: revulsion against the radical politics of the past which had embraced, and sustained for far too long, the power of an over-ambitious, self-seeking tyrant whose dictatorship – notwithstanding years of military triumph and the prestige thereby bestowed upon the nation – ultimately led a great nation to humiliation and ruin.

It is important to explain these circumstances in concrete terms – to demonstrate exactly what Allied victory/French defeat at Waterloo actually meant – and to stress that its consequences and legacy must not be seen in isolation; that is, as an event without a past. As the last battle of the Napoleonic Wars, Waterloo marked a culmination of events – the end of an era which had begun at least as early as the Revolution in 1789, but certainly no later than the start of the wars which that movement had spawned, three years later. Thus, to assess the significance of Waterloo is to assess the French Revolutionary and Napoleonic Wars as a whole.

*Pensioners at the Royal Hospital, Chelsea reading news of the battle.*

## NAMING THE BATTLE

Upon greeting Wellington after the battle, Blücher proposed to call the engagement 'La Belle Alliance' after the place where the two commanders met. Appreciating, however, that his countrymen would find the name too difficult to pronounce, the duke instead chose 'Waterloo', after the site of his headquarters. Precise accuracy suggests 'Mont St Jean', for the village of Waterloo did not in fact figure in the fighting.

The wars which stretched from 1792 to 1815 demonstrated that only by concerted action could the Great Powers of Europe expect to defeat the overwhelming power of France, a point that ought to have been appreciated before 1941 by the United States and the Soviet Union. Moreover, by 1814 the Allies had come to the correct conclusion that peace would be short-lived, unless they maintained a system of collaboration whereby the rights of states were respected and force became a last resort in the exercise of power. By adhering to these principles, peace prevailed for two generations – an unprecedented course of events in the modern era. The arrangements reached at the Congress of Vienna, which reconvened after Waterloo, marked the beginning of a new phase in international relations for, although flawed, the delegates' collective work produced a broadly accepted compromise, putting paid to the complex system of temporary alliances dating back to the formation of the First Coalition in 1792 which, owing to its failure, brought forth six more coalitions (the Waterloo campaign of course constituting the seventh) of varying strength and a host of other minor alliances in the quest for victory over France. In this respect, the Vienna settlement proved a panacea to the long eighteenth-century tradition of warfare waged on a regular basis between antagonists whose alliances shifted as and when their interests dictated.

To reach that point, however, significant costs in human life were involved, even when examining the losses of only two of the (albeit principal) combatants, Britain and France. Notwithstanding Britain's physical isolation and the protection from invasion offered by her naval superiority – in addition to the fact that the army, although heavily engaged in Iberia, did not suffer the heavy costs of the long, attritional struggles endured by her continental counterparts – she still lost about 220,000 soldiers and sailors, only a tenth of whom perished as a consequence of combat, the remaining falling victim to sickness and disease. One may be surprised to learn that losses on this scale, as a proportion of Britain's population, closely resembled those of the First World War. Overall, the Napoleonic Wars alone are thought to have caused at least 900,000 military deaths across Europe, translated into a mortality rate for those males born between 1790 and 1795 of nearly 40 per cent. If to this figure is added civilian deaths, the number rises to perhaps 5 million, or roughly the same proportion of the European population lost in the conflict of 1914–18

*Wellington and Blücher salute one another upon meeting. Their failure to anticipate an early attack by Napoleon constituted the first potentially grave strategic error committed by the Allies in a campaign which, but for a series of even greater French blunders, might have ended very differently indeed.*

– an extraordinary statistic when one considers the yawning technological gaps which separate the two conflicts, albeit the First World War covering a much more confined period of time.

The Revolutionary and Napoleonic Wars ushered in the modern state – a fact which the outcome of Waterloo simply could not reverse – for although in 1815 the ruling classes who had been divested of power restored the former style of government wherever possible, their predecessors' efforts at centralising power and fashioning a more efficient government bureaucracy remained in place and generally found favour with the new regimes. Together with greater centralisation of power, a number of states in 1815 found themselves physically enlarged, for the treaties of Paris and the agreements reached at Vienna consolidated territorial holdings in far fewer hands than had been the case in 1792. This greatly simplified the political map of Europe and created several monolithic states, such as Austria and Prussia, with very few non-contiguous territories – in sharp contrast to the pre-war era when the Austrian Netherlands and many parts of the (Prussian-controlled) Rhineland lay well beyond the immediate protection and administration of their masters. In addition, a number of the small German states of the former Holy Roman Empire were of sufficient size to become considerably more economically viable than their predecessors and could now mount respectable armed forces in their own right, particularly Bavaria.

As a result of Waterloo if, in many though not all cases, dynasties and individual rulers were restored to their former possessions – though much rationalisation of the map in light of two decades of change was required – this could not entirely alter the fact that subjects had experienced a taste of republicanism, such that the concept of 'the people' could not pass altogether ignored. Feudalism, the system of serfs owing allegiance to local landowners, which had been abolished in France under the Revolution and in most of the rest of Europe by 1808, was not re-instated. Nevertheless, the aristocracy for the most part re-asserted itself socially and politically – certainly in France, but in German territories as well – despite the reforms introduced and in many cases firmly ensconced by enemy occupation. Yet, at least for the next fifteen years, there was no significant backlash or violent reaction, partly as a result of the growing desire of the middle classes for social mobility; in short, those of a bourgeois disposition were hardly prepared to undermine the power of the upper classes, when it was their social, political and economic status to which the middle class aspired. Indeed, the two regarded themselves as natural allies, looking upon those socially inferior to themselves as a potential threat to the status quo and, above all, to the stable political order ushered in by peace. So far as they were concerned the masses were not to be loathed, but on the other hand certainly not to be trusted either, and thus the forms of liberal government which had proliferated among the German states of the Confederation of the Rhine, the Low Countries

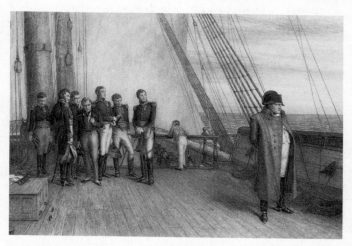

British naval officers study their prisoner aboard HMS Bellerophon. By exiling the emperor to St Helena and establishing a permanent guard over him on land as well as at sea, his captors sought to eradicate all possibility of another Napoleonic bid for power. Sir Hudson Lowe, the island's commander, refused to recognise Napoleon's imperial title, instead addressing him only as 'General Bonaparte', thereby acknowledging his military, but not his political, authority.

and northern and central Italy, gave way to more limited forms of representative government, to the extent that the dramatic inroads made by republicanism since the outbreak of the wars in 1792 faced powerful reactionary forces. Having said this, Allied victory at Waterloo simply could not turn the clock back entirely.

Waterloo at last enabled the victorious powers to recast Europe on the basis originally sought when the Congress of Vienna first met the previous year – though in light of Napoleon's new bid for power in 1815, and in contrast to the atmosphere prevailing in the spring of 1814, the Allies were no longer seeking conciliation or to welcome France back into the community of nations on a more-or-less equal basis. Rather, theirs was to be a transparently punitive peace, with conditions far harsher than those contained in the first Treaty of Paris on 30 May 1814. Accordingly, the Allies established and fixed new frontiers in the wake of more than two decades of upheaval, with the principal decisions made – as at Versailles a hundred years later – by the principal victors: in this case Britain, Russia, Austria and Prussia. There is no question that Britain's decisive contribution to French defeat at Waterloo immensely strengthened her hand in these affairs. Thus, what contemporaries identified as the 'Great Powers', including Britain, established a series of buffer states around France for the purpose of creating a defensive ring to discourage future forays. To this end, they established a new United Kingdom of the Netherlands, consisting of what today constitutes Holland, Belgium and Luxembourg; a German Confederation, which greatly reduced the number of independent states in central Europe from the several hundred of the early 1790s to a much more manageable thirty-nine.

To the southeast, the kingdom of Lombardy-Venetia was established under the control of the Austrian emperor – again as a buffer against any renewed French efforts in pursuit of territorial aggrandisement. In the east, Poland, having been partitioned three times in the 1770s and '90s and making a brief revival in the form of the Napoleonic satellite state, the Duchy of Warsaw, was replaced by 'Congress Poland', a kingdom under Tsar Alexander.

As Russia thus expanded west and the Austrians extended into Italy and re-established control over the Dalmatian coast, Prussia could not go uncompensated, acquiring territory in Westphalia, Pomerania and Saxony. The settlement of 1815 also rewarded Sweden with the cession of Norway, while Britain retained Cape Colony in southern Africa, Ceylon, Mauritius, St Lucia, Tobago and Malta, with a protectorate over the Ionian Islands in the Aegean. Switzerland became officially neutral from this time and the former dynasties ousted from across Europe for the most part re-established themselves, with efforts made to restore the privileges once enjoyed by their royalist supporters. Thus, the former monarchies resumed control in Spain, Sardinia, Naples, Tuscany and Modena. France was reduced to her frontiers of 1790, with territorial concessions granted to Prussia, Bavaria, Piedmont-Sardinia, and the Netherlands in the form of part of Savoy and the whole of Philippeville, Marienburg, Saarlouis and Landau. France was to pay an indemnity of 700,000 francs and accept the military occupation of seventeen of her fortresses, at her own expense, for three years.

Quite apart from performing the task of keeping a watch along the Rhine against future French expansion, the heads of state and diplomats assembled at Vienna inadvertently established the basis for future German unification – albeit a circumstance not realised until 1871 – not just as a result of the simplification of central European frontiers, but also as a consequence of the recently unleashed forces of nationalism, particularly those encouraged by the French occupation of Prussia between 1807 and 1813. In short, the antagonisms engendered by the conqueror went far in encouraging Germans to regard themselves as a single people rather than a disparate group who, though sharing a common language and culture (albeit divided between the Protestant north and the Catholic south), continued to adhere to regional, parochial allegiances, such as to the local potentate or ecclesiastical state.

In France, while the Bourbons might once again mount the throne in Paris they could not entirely reverse what had been

*Wearing their distinctive bearskin caps, Imperial Guardsmen stand in square. Effectively unbreakable against cavalry, this formation offered a magnificent target to artillery, particularly to gunners employing canister or case shot at short range.*

achieved on the political front, and thus had to settle again, as before Waterloo, for a constitutional monarchy not unlike that which existed in Britain at the time. This was broadly acceptable to the Allies, who understood that the old dynasty and a new constitution, though not entirely palatable, would have to be tolerated lest its abolition unleash the revolutionary ferment which had plunged Europe into war in the first place. Indeed, many of the reforms instituted during the wars remained and, in many cases, found welcoming adherents among the new elites – not least the Napoleonic Code (*Code Napoléon*), which greatly simplified the old, immensely complex legal system of the royalist era. Many of those new to power also embraced the machinery of the administrative structure introduced by the revolutionaries and later improved upon by Napoleon, who had also established a stable financial base for the nation. Many reforms, which championed equality before the law, the right of land ownership, and protection for private property, particularly benefitted the middle classes and contributed to the sort of social and political stability sought by those newly restored to power. While trampling

## NAPOLEON'S FATE AFTER WATERLOO

Once he appreciated that he could not reverse the tide of fortune, Napoleon abdicated a second time and abandoned Paris in a bid either to escape to America, a project which failed when he found French ports under blockade or, astonishingly enough, to live in comfortable exile in Britain. On 15 July, surrendering himself to the captain of HMS *Bellerophon*, then cruising off La Rochelle, Napoleon failed to appreciate the consequences of his action, for British authorities, determined to ensure that he never again threaten European security, exiled him to the remote South Atlantic island of St Helena, where he died six years later.

upon such reforms may have appealed to those of a more reactionary disposition, most of them appreciated the adoption of a pragmatic approach: a tolerance for the new order of things in recognition of the unimpeachable fact that an irreversible social revolution had taken place during their long absence in exile.

Napoleon's defeat at Waterloo – or the Allies' victory, depending on one's perspective – could not reverse the profound impact which France had upon the conquered states of Europe, no more so than in the territories which France had incorporated directly into the empire, thereby ensuring that the impact of Napoleonic influence remained strong until the closing days of the emperor's reign. In the Low Countries, the Rhineland and other small German states, and even as far away as Naples, the Napoleonic Code persisted for many years virtually untouched or, where diluted, continued to make an impact until well into the twentieth century – and in some cases continues to prevail as the legal norm through to the present day. Other Napoleonic institutions remained substantially as the emperor had left them upon his final exile, such as the police service, the system of taxation, and the political and religious accommodation made with the Catholic Church, known as the Concordat. Moreover, if the Napoleonic army was recast under the Bourbons to efface many of the changes instituted under the Empire, this was less the case with France's neighbours, many of whom continued to maintain armed forces organised, trained and equipped in the style of their former masters.

Finally, the wars had demonstrated that the era of manoeuvre for the sake of attaining a limited advantage over one's opponent in the quest for a negotiated settlement – such as for the acquisition of a set of fortresses or a narrow strip of territory – had come to a close. War, in the manner practiced both by the revolutionaries and by Napoleon, now determined the fate of nations. Armies were to seek battle, not avoid it – with Waterloo merely the last of many dozens like it in scale, particularly since Austerlitz in 1805 – with the expressed intention of destroying the enemy's main force in pursuit of a decisive and long-term political result. Nothing marked the break between Napoleon's manner of waging war and that of his eighteenth-century predecessors more than the concept of wielding the army as a political instrument for the sake of recasting the vanquished as a vassal state or refashioning it as an ally prepared to support the conqueror's ambition of expanding his power and dominion in an endless quest for glory.

# ORDERS OF BATTLE

*Armée du Nord*
(Emperor Napoleon)

(At Waterloo: 77,500 men
and 246 guns)

## Imperial Guard (Lieutenant General *Comte* Drouot)

*Lieutenant General Comte
Friant*
1st and 2nd Grenadiers
*Lieutenant General Comte
Roguet*
3rd and 4th Grenadiers
*Lieutenant General Comte
Morand*
1st and 2nd Chasseurs
*Lieutenant General Comte
Michel*
3rd and 4th Chasseurs
*Lieutenant General Comte
Duhesme*
1st and 3rd Tirailleurs
*Lieutenant General Comte
Barrois*
1st and 3rd Voltigeurs
*Lieutenant General Lefebvre-
Desnöettes*
Lancers and Chasseurs à
Cheval
*Lieutenant General Comte Guyot*
Dragoons, Grenadiers à
Cheval and Gendarmerie
d'Elite
*Lieutenant General Desvaux de
St Maurice*
9 batteries, Guard Foot
Artillery; 4 batteries,
Guard Horse Artillery;
Marines of the Guard;
Engineers of the Guard

## I Corps (Lieutenant General Jean Baptiste Drouet, *Comte* d'Erlon)

*1st Division
(Lieutenant General Baron
Quiot du Passage)*

*1st Brigade (Brigadier General
Quiot)*
54th and 55th Légère
*2nd Brigade (Brigadier General
Bourgeois)*
28th and 105th Ligne

**2nd Division**
*(Lieutenant General Baron Donzelot)*

*1st Brigade (Brigadier General Schmitz)*
13th Légère; 17th Ligne
*2nd Brigade (Brigadier General Baron Aulard)*
19th and 31st Ligne

**3rd Division**
*(Lieutenant General Baron Marcognet)*

*1st Brigade (Brigadier General Noguès)*
21st and 46th Ligne

**4th Division**
*(Lieutenant General Comte Durutte)*

*1st Brigade (Brigadier General Pegot)*
8th and 29th Ligne
*2nd Brigade (Brigadier General Brue)*
85th and 95th Ligne

*1st Cavalry Division*
*(Lieutenant General Baron Jaquinot)*

*1st Brigade (Brigadier General Bruno)*
7th Hussars and 3rd Chasseurs à Cheval
*2nd Brigade (Brigadier General Baron Gobrecht)*
3rd and 4th Lancers

Artillery: 5 batteries, Foot Artillery; 1 battery, Horse Artillery; Engineers

# II Corps
**(Lieutenant General *Comte* Honoré Charles Reille)**

**5th Division**
*(Lieutenant General Baron Bachelu)*

*1st Brigade (Brigadier General Baron Husson)*
2nd Légère, 61st Ligne
*2nd Brigade (Brigadier General Baron Campi)*
72nd and 108th Ligne

**6th Division**
*(Lieutenant General Prince Jerome Napoleon)*

*1st Brigade (Brigadier General Baron Baudouin)*
1st Légère and 3rd Ligne
*2nd Brigade (Brigadier General Soye)*
1st and 2nd Légère

**7th Division**
*(Lieutenant General Comte Girard)*

*1st Brigade (Brigadier General de Villiers)*
11th Légère, 82nd Ligne
*2nd Brigade (Brigadier General Baron Piat)*
12th Légère, 4th Ligne

**9th Division**
*(Lieutenant General Comte Foy)*

*1st Brigade (Brigadier General Baron Gauthier)*
92nd and 93rd Ligne
*2nd Brigade (Brigadier General Jamin)*
4th Légère, 100th Ligne

*2nd Cavalry Division*
*(Lieutenant General Piré)*

*1st Brigade (Brigadier General Baron Hubert)*
1st and 6th Chasseurs à Cheval

2nd Brigade (Brigadier General Baron Wathiez)
>> 5th and 6th Lancers

Artillery: 5 batteries, Foot Artillery; 1 battery, Horse Artillery; Engineers

## III Corps
## (Lieutenant General *Comte* Vandamme (at Wavre))

*8th Division (Lieutenant General Baron Lefol)*

1st Brigade (Brigadier General Baron Billiard)
>> 15th Légère, 23rd Ligne

2nd Brigade (Brigadier General Baron Corsin)
>> 37th and 64th Ligne

*10th Division (Lieutenant General Baron Habert)*

1st Brigade (Brigadier General Gengoult)
>> 34th and 88th Ligne

2nd Brigade (Brigadier General Dupeyroux)
>> 22nd and 70th Ligne, 2nd Swiss Regiment

*11th Division (Lieutenant General Baron Berthezène)*

1st Brigade (Brigadier General Dufour)
>> 12th and 56th Ligne

2nd Brigade (Brigadier General Baron Lagarde)
>> 33rd and 86th Ligne

*3rd Cavalry Division (Lieutenant General Baron Domon)*

1st Brigade (Brigadier General Baron Dommanget)
>> 4th and 9th Chasseurs à Cheval

2nd Brigade (Brigadier General Baron Vinot)
>> 12th Chasseurs à Cheval

Artillery: 4 batteries, Foot Artillery; 1 battery, Horse Artillery; Engineers

## IV Corps
## (Lieutenant General *Comte* Gérard (at Wavre))

*12th Division (Lieutenant General Comte Pêcheux)*

1st Brigade (Brigadier General Rome)
>> 30th and 96th Ligne

2nd Brigade (Brigadier General Baron Shoeffer)
>> 6th Légère, 63rd Ligne

*13th Division (Lieutenant General Baron Vichery)*

1st Brigade (Brigadier General Baron le Capitaine)
>> 59th and 76th Ligne

2nd Brigade (Brigadier General Desprez)
>> 48th and 69th Ligne

*14th Division (Lieutenant General Hulot)*

1st Brigade
>> 9th Légère, 111th Ligne

2nd Brigade (Brigadier General Toussaint)
>> 44th and 50th Ligne

*7th Cavalry Division (Lieutenant General Baron Maurin)*

1st Brigade (Brigadier General Baron Vallin)
6th Hussars, 8th Chasseurs à Cheval

2nd Brigade (Brigadier General Berruyer)
6th, 11th and 16th Dragoons

Artillery: 4 batteries, Foot Artillery; 1 battery, Horse Artillery; Engineers

# VI Corps
# (Gen de Div, *Comte* de Lobau)

*19th Division*
*(Lieutenant General Baron Simmer)*

1st Brigade (Brigadier General Baron de Bellair)
5th and 11th Ligne

2nd Brigade (Brigadier General Jamin)
27th and 84th Ligne

*20th Division*
*(Lieutenant General Baron Jeanin)*

1st Brigade (Brigadier General Bony)
5th Légère, 10th Ligne

2nd Brigade (Brigadier General de Tromelin)
107th Ligne

*21st Division*
*(Lieutenant General Baron Teste)*

1st Brigade (Brigadier General Baron Lafitte)
8th Légère

2nd Brigade (Brigadier General Baron Penne)
65th and 75th Ligne

Artillery: 4 batteries, Foot Artillery; 1 battery, Horse Artillery; Engineers

# I Cavalry Corps
# (Lieutenant General *Comte* Pajol)

*4th Cavalry Division*
*(Lieutenant General Baron Soult)*

1st Brigade (Brigadier General St Laurent)
1st and 4th Hussars

2nd Brigade (Brigadier General Ameil)
5th Hussars

*5th Cavalry Division*
*(Lieutenant General Baron Subervie)*

1st Brigade (Brigadier General de Colbert)
1st and 2nd Lancers

2nd Brigade (Brigadier General Merlin de Douai)
11th Chasseurs à Cheval

Artillery: 2 batteries, Horse Artillery

# II Cavalry Corps
# (Lieutenant General *Comte* Exelmans)

*9th Cavalry Division*
*(Lieutenant General Baron Strolz)*

1st Brigade (Brigadier General Baron Burthe)
5th and 13th Dragoons

2nd Brigade (Brigadier General Baron Vincent)
15th and 20th Dragoons

*10th Cavalry Division*
*(Lieutenant General Baron Chastel)*

1st Brigade (Brigadier General Baron Bennemains)

    4th and 12th Dragoons

2nd Brigade (Brigadier General Berton)

    14th and 17th Dragoons

Artillery: 2 batteries, Horse Artillery

## III Cavalry Corps (Lieutenant General Kellerman)

11th Cavalry Division (Lieutenant General Baron L'Héritier)

1st Brigade (Brigadier General Baron Picquet)

    2nd and 7th Dragoons

2nd Brigade (Brigadier General Baron Guiton)

    8th and 11th Cuirassiers

12th Cavalry Division (Lieutenant General Roussel d'Hurbal)

1st Brigade (Brigadier General Baron Blanchard)

    1st and 2nd Carabiniers

2nd Brigade (Brigadier General Donop)

    2nd and 3rd Cuirassiers

Artillery: 2 batteries, Horse Artillery

## IV Cavalry Corps (Lieutenant General Comte Milhaud)

13th Cavalry Division (Lieutenant General Wathier)

1st Brigade (Brigadier General Baron Dubois)

    1st and 4th Cuirassiers

2nd Brigade (Brigadier General Travers)

    7th and 12th Cuirassiers

14th Cavalry Division (Lieutenant General Baron Delort)

1st Brigade (Brigadier General Baron Vial)

    5th and 10th Cuirassiers

2nd Brigade (Brigadier General Baron Farine)

    6th and 9th Cuirassiers

Artillery: 2 batteries, Horse Artillery

Total strength:

|  | At Waterloo | At Wavre | Total |
| --- | --- | --- | --- |
| Infantry | 53,400 | 24,000 | 77,400 |
| Cavalry | 15,600 | 3,500 | 19,100 |
| Artillery & Train | 6,500 | 2,000 | 8,500 |
| Others* | 2,000 | 500 | 2,500 |
| Totals | 77,500 | 30,000 | 107,500 |
| Guns | 246 | 96 | 342 +8 at Ligny |

*Includes HQ Staff; regimental staffs included in infantry and cavalry statistics above.

# Anglo-Allied Army (Field Marshal the Duke of Wellington)

(At Waterloo: 73,200 men and 157 guns + 1 rocket bty)

## I Corps
### (The Prince of Orange)

*1st Division*
*(Major General Cooke)*

*1st British Brigade (Major General Maitland)*
1st and 3rd Battalions, 1st Foot Guards
*2nd British Brigade (Major General Sir J. Byng)*
2nd Battalion, 2nd Foot Guards; 2nd Battalion, 3rd Foot Guards

Artillery (Lieutenant Colonel Adye): 1 Foot battery, Royal Artillery; 1 Horse Artillery battery, King's German Legion

*3rd Division Lieutenant (General Sir Charles Alten)*

*5th British Brigade (Major General Sir C. Halkett)*
2nd Battalion, 30th Foot; 33rd Foot; 2nd Battalion, 69th Foot; 2nd Battalion, 73rd Foot
*2nd King's German Legion Brigade (Colonel von Ompteda)*
1st and 2nd Light Battalions; 5th and 8th Line Battalions
*1st Hanoverian Brigade (Major General Count Kielmannsegge)*
Field-Battalions Bremen, Verden and York; Light Battalions Lüneburg and Grubenhagen; Field-Jäger Corps

Artillery (Lieutenant Colonel Williamson): 1 Foot battery, Royal Artillery; 1 Foot battery, King's German Legion

*2nd Netherlands Division (Lieutenant General Baron de Perponcher)*

*1st Brigade (Major General Count Bylandt)*
7th Infantry; 27th Jägers; 5th, 7th and 8th Militia
*2nd Brigade (Prince Bernhard of Saxe-Weimar)*
2nd Nassau Regiment; Regiment of Orange Nassau

Artillery (Major van Opstal): 1 battery, Horse Artillery; 1 battery, Foot Artillery

*3rd Netherlands Division (Lieutenant General Baron Chassé)*

*1st Brigade (Major General Ditmers)*
2nd Infantry; 35th Jägers; 4th, 6th, 17th and 19th Militia
*2nd Brigade (Major General d'Aubremé)*
3rd, 12th and 13th Infantry; 36th Jägers; 3rd and 10th Militia

Artillery (Major van der Smissen): 1 battery, Horse Artillery; 1 battery, Foot Artillery

## II Corps
## (Lieutenant General Lord Hill)

### 2nd Division
### (Lieutenant General Sir H. Clinton)

3rd British Brigade (Major General Adam)
: 1st Battalion, 52nd Light Infantry; 1st Battalion, 71st Light Infantry; 2nd and 3rd Battalions, 95th Rifles

1st King's German Legion Brigade (Colonel du Plat)
: 1st, 2nd, 3rd and 4th Line Battalions

3rd Hanoverian Brigade (Colonel H. Halkett)
: Landwehr Battalions Bremervörde, Osnabrück, Quackenbrück and Salzgitter

Artillery (Lieutenant Colonel Gold): 1 battery, Foot Artillery, Royal Artillery; 1 Horse Artillery battery, King's German Legion

### 4th Division
### (Lieutenant General Sir Charles Colville)

4th British Brigade (Colonel Mitchell)
: 3rd Battalion, 14th Foot; 1st Battalion, 23rd Fusiliers; 51st Light Infantry

6th British Brigade (Major General Johnstone)
: 2nd Battalion, 35th Foot; 1st Battalion, 54th Foot; 2nd Btn, 59th Foot; 1st Battalion, 91st Foot

6th Hanoverian Brigade (Major General Sir J. Lyon)
: Field-Battalions Lauenberg and Calenberg; Landwehr Battalions Nienburg, Hoya and Bentheim

Artillery (Lieutenant Colonel Hawker): 1 battery, Foot Artillery, Royal Artillery; 1 battery, Foot Artillery, King's German Legion

### 1st Netherlands Division
### (Lieutenant General Stedmann)

1st Brigade (Major General Hauw)
: 4th and 6th Infantry; 16th Jägers; 9th, 14th and 15th Militia

2nd Brigade (Major General Eerens)
: 1st Infantry; 18th Jägers; 1st, 2nd and 18th Militia

Artillery: 1 battery, Foot Artillery

Netherlands Indian Brigade (Lieutenant General Anthing)
: 5th Infantry; Battalion of Flanquers; 10th and 11th Jägers; 1 battery, Foot Artillery Reserve

### 5th Division
### (Lieutenant General Sir T. Picton)

8th British Brigade (Major General Sir J. Kempt)
: 1st Battalion, 28th Foot; 1st Battalion, 32nd Foot; 1st Battalion, 79th Highlanders; 1st Battalion, 95th Rifles

9th British Brigade (Major General Sir D. Pack)

3rd Battalion, 1st Foot;
1st Battalion, 42nd
Highlanders; 2nd
Battalion, 44th Foot;
1st Battalion, 92nd
Highlanders
*5th Hanoverian Brigade (Colonel von Vincke)*
Landwehr Btns Hameln,
Gifhorn, Peine and
Hildesheim

Artillery (Major Heisse): 1 battery,
Foot Artillery, Royal Artillery; 1
battery, Foot Artillery, Hanoverian
Artillery

*6th Division
(Lieutenant General Hon. Sir L. Cole)*

*10th British Brigade (Major General Sir J. Lambert)*
1st Battalion, 4th Foot; 1st
Battalion, 27th Foot; 1st
Battalion, 40th Foot; 2nd
Battalion, 81st Foot
*4th Hanoverian Brigade (Colonel Best)*
Landwehr Battalions
Lüneburg, Verden,
Osterode and Münden

Artillery (Lieutenant Colonel
Brückmann): 2 batteries, Foot
Artillery, Royal Artillery
British Reserve Artillery (Major
Drummond): 2 batteries, Royal Horse
Artillery; 3 batteries, Royal Foot
Artillery

*7th Division*

*7th British Brigade*
2nd Battalion, 25th Foot;
2nd Battalion, 37th Foot;
2nd Battalion, 78th Foot

*British Garrison Troops*
13th Veteran Battalion;
2nd Garrison Battalion; 1st
Foreign Battalion

*Brunswick Corps
(Duke of Brunswick)*

*Advanced Guard Battalion (Major von Rauschenplatt)*

*Light Brigade (Lieutenant Colonel von Buttlar)*
Guard Battalion; 1st, 2nd
and 3rd Light Battalions
*Line Brigade (Lieutenant Colonel von Specht)*
1st, 2nd and 3rd Line
Battalions

Artillery (Major Mahn): 1 battery,
Horse Artillery; 1 battery, Foot Artillery

*Hanoverian Reserve Corps
(Lieutenant General von der Decken)*

*1st Brigade (Lieutenant Colonel von Bennigsen)*
Field-Battalion Hoya;
Landwehr Battalions Mölln
and Bremerlehe
*2nd Brigade (Lieutenant Colonel von Beaulieu)*
Landwehr Battalions
Nordheim, Ahlefeldt and
Springe
*3rd Brigade (Lieutenant Colonel Bodecker)*
Landwehr Battalions
Otterndorf, Zelle and
Ratzeburg
*4th Brigade (Lieutenant Colonel Wissel)*
Landwehr Battalions
Hanover, Uelzen, Neustadt
and Diepholz

*Nassau Contingent
(General von Kruse)*

*1st Infantry*

*1st British Brigade (Major General Lord Somerset)*
 1st and 2nd Life Guards; Royal Horse Guards; 1st Dragoon Guards
*2nd British Brigade (Major General Sir W. Ponsonby)*
 1st, 2nd and 6th Dragoons
*3rd British Brigade (Major General Sir W. Dörnberg)*
 23rd Light Dragoons; 1st and 2nd Light Dragoons, King's German Legion
*4th British Brigade (Major General Sir J. Vandeleur)*
 11th, 12th and 16th Light Dragoons
*5th British Brigade (Major General Sir C. Grant)*
 7th and 15th Hussars; 2nd Hussars, King's German Legion
*6th British Brigade (Major General Sir H. Vivian)*
 10th and 18th Hussars; 1st Hussars, King's German Legion
*7th British Brigade (Colonel Sir F. von Arentsschildt)*
 13th Light Dragoons; 3rd Hussars, King's German Legion

*British Horse Artillery (attached to the cavalry)*
 5 batteries, Royal Horse Artillery; 1 battery, Mounted Rocket Corps
*1st Hanoverian Brigade (Colonel von Estorff)*
 *Prince Regent's Hussars; Bremen and Verden Hussars; Duke of Cumberland's Hussars*
*Cavalry of the Brunswick Corps*
 *Regiment of Hussars; Regiment of Uhlans*
*1st Netherlands Brigade (Major General Trip)*
 *1st and 3rd Dutch Carabiniers; 2nd Belgian Carabiniers*
*2nd Netherlands Brigade (Major General de Ghigny)*
 *4th Dutch Light Dragoons; 8th Belgian Hussars*
*3rd Netherlands Brigade (Major General van Merlen)*
 *5th Belgian Light Dragoons; 6th Dutch Hussars*

Netherlands Horse Artillery (attached to the cavalry): 2 half-batteries; Engineers, etc. (All British units): Corps of Royal Engineers; Corps of Royal Sappers and Miners; Royal Waggon Train; Royal Staff Corps

Total strength of Anglo-Allied Army:

|           | At Waterloo | At Hal and Tubize | Total  |
|-----------|-------------|-------------------|--------|
| Infantry  | 53,850      | 15,000            | 68,850 |
| Cavalry   | 13,350      | 1,200             | 14,550 |
| Artillery | 5,000       | 700               | 5,700  |
| Others*   | 1,000       | 100               | 1,100  |
| Totals    | 73,200      | 17,000            | 90,200 |

Guns     157 + 1 section of rockets
* Sappers, Miners, Staff Corps, HQ Staff, etc.

# Prussian Army of the Lower Rhine
# (Field Marshal Gebhard Leberecht von Blücher)

(At Waterloo: 49,000 men and 134 guns)

## I Corps
## (Lieutenant General Count Hans von Ziethen)

*1st Brigade (General Steinmetz)*
12th and 24th Infantry; 1st Westphalian Landwehr; 1st and 3rd Silesian Jäger Companies
*2nd Brigade (General von Pirch II)*
6th and 28th Infantry; 2nd Westphalian Landwehr
*3rd Brigade (General von Jagow)*
7th and 29th Infantry; 3rd Westphalian Landwehr; 2nd and 4th Silesian Jäger Companies
*4th Brigade (General von Henkel)*
19th Infantry;

4th Westphalian Landwehr Cavalry (Lieutenant General von Röder)
*Brigade of General von Treskow*
2nd and 5th Dragoons; Brandenburg Uhlans
*Brigade of Lieutenant Colonel von Lützow*
6th Uhlans; 1st and 2nd Kurmark Landwehr Cavalry; 1st Silesian Hussars; 1st Westphalian Landwehr Cavalry

Artillery (Colonel von Lehmann): 3 12lb Foot batteries; 5 6lb Foot batteries; 1 Howitzer battery; 3 Horse Artillery batteries

## II Corps
## (Major General von Pirch I)

*1st Brigade (General von Tippelskirchen)*
2nd and 25th Infantry; 5th Westphalian Landwehr
*6th Brigade (General von Krafft)*
9th and 26th Infantry; 1st Elbe Landwehr

*7th Brigade (General von Brause)*
14th and 22nd Infantry;
2nd Elbe Landwehr
*8th Brigade (Colonel von Langen)*
21st and 23rd Infantry;
3rd Elbe Landwehr

*Cavalry*
*General von Jürgass*

*Brigade of Colonel Von Thümen*
Silesian Uhlans; 6th
Dragoons; 11th Hussars
*Brigade of Colonel Count Schulenburg*
1st Dragoons; 4th
Kurmark Landwehr
Cavalry
*Brigade of Lieutenant Colonel von Sohr*
3rd and 5th Hussars;
5th Kurmark Landwehr
Cavalry; Elbe Landwehr
Cavalry

Artillery (Colonel Von Röhl): 2 12lb
Foot batteries; 5 6lb Foot batteries;
3 Horse Artillery batteries

## III Corps
## (Lieutenant General von Thielemann (at Wavre))

*9th Brigade (General von Borcke)*
8th and 36th Infantry;
1st Kurmark Landwehr
*10th Brigade (Colonel von Kämpfen)*
27th Infantry; 2nd
Kurmark Landwehr
*11th Brigade (Colonel von Luck)*
3rd and 4th Kurmark
Landwehr
*12th Brigade (Colonel von Stülpnagel)*

31st Infantry; 5th and
6th Kurmark Landwehr

*Cavalry (General von Hobe)*

*Brigade of Colonel von der Marwitz*
7th and 8th Uhlans; 9th
Hussars
*Brigade of Colonel Count Lottum*
5th Uhlans; 7th
Dragoons; 3rd and 6th
Kurmark Landwehr
Cavalry

Artillery (Colonel von Mohnhaupt):
1 12lb Foot battery; 2 6lb Foot
Artillery batteries; 3 Horse Artillery
batteries

## IV Corps
## (General Count Friedrich Wilhelm Bülow von Dennewitz)

*13th Brigade (Lieutenant General von Hacke)*
10th Infantry; 2nd and
3rd Neumark Landwehr
*14th Brigade (General von Ryssel)*
11th Infantry; 1st
and 2nd Pomeranian
Landwehr
*15th Brigade (General von Losthin)*
18th Infantry; 3rd and
4th Silesian Landwehr
*16th Brigade (Colonel Hiller von Gartringen)*
15th Infantry; 1st and
2nd Silesian Landwehr

*Cavalry*
*(General Prince William of Prussia)*

# Waterloo 1815

*Brigade of General von Sydow*
    1st Uhlans; 2nd and 8th Hussars

*Brigade of Colonel Count Schwerin*
    10th Hussars; 1st and 2nd Neumark Landwehr Cavalry; 1st and 2nd Pomeranian Landwehr Cavalry

*Brigade of Lieutenant Colonel von Watzdorf*
    1st, 2nd and 3rd Silesian Landwehr Cavalry

Artillery (Lieutenant Colonel von Bardeleben): 3 12lb Foot batteries; 5 6lb Foot batteries; 3 Horse Artillery batteries

Total strength (approximately):

|           | At Waterloo | En route | At Wavre | Total   |
|-----------|-------------|----------|----------|---------|
| Infantry  | 38,000      | 20,300   | 20,000   | 78,300  |
| Cavalry   | 7,000       | 3,000    | 3,000    | 13,000  |
| Artillery | 2,500       | 2,000    | 1,250    | 5,750   |
| Others*   | 1,500       | 1,000    | 750      | 3,250   |
| Totals    | 49,000      | 26,300   | 25,000   | 100,300 |
| Guns      | 134         | 106      | 43       | 283     |

# FURTHER READING

Adkin, Mark, *The Waterloo Companion: The Complete Guide to History's Most Famous Land Battle* (London: Aurum, 2001)

Barbero, Alessandro, *The Battle: A New History of the Battle of Waterloo* (London: Atlantic Books, 2005)

Bernard, Giles, and Gérard Lachaux, *Waterloo* (Paris: Histoire and Collections, 2005)

Black, Jeremy, *The Battle of Waterloo: A New History* (London: Icon Books, 2010)

Bowden, Scott, *Armies at Waterloo* (Arlington, TX: Emperor's Press, 1983)

Brett-James, Antony, *The Hundred Days* (London: Macmillan, 1964)

Chalfont, Lord (ed.) *Waterloo: The Hundred Days* (London: Sedgwick and Jackson, 1979)

Chandler, David, *The Campaigns of Napoleon* (London: Weidenfeld and Nicolson, 1995)

—, (ed.) *Napoleon's Marshals* (London: Cassell, 2000)

—, *Waterloo: The Hundred Days* (New York: Macmillan, 1981)

Chapman, Tim, *The Congress of Vienna: Origins, Process and Results* (New York: Routledge, 1998)

Chesney, Charles, *Waterloo Lectures* (London: Greenhill, [1907] 1997)

Corrigan, Gordon, *Wellington: A Military Life* (London: Hambledown Continuum, 2001)

Coss, Edward, *All for the King's Shilling: The British Army under Wellington, 1808–1814* (Oklahoma: University of Oklahoma Press, 2010)

Dallas, Gregor, *The Final Act: The Roads to Waterloo* (New York: Holt, 1997)

Davies, Paul, *The Field of Waterloo* (London: Pan Books, 1971)

Elting, John, *Swords Around a Throne: Napoleon's Grande Armée* (London: Weidenfield and Nicolson, 1997)

Ferrero, Guglielmo, *The Reconstruction of Europe: Talleyrand and the Congress of Vienna, 1814–1815* (New York: Norton, 1963)

Fletcher, Ian, *A Desperate Business: Wellington, the British Army and the Waterloo Campaign* (Staplehurst: Spellmount, 2003)

—, *Galloping at Everything: The British Cavalry in the Peninsular War and at Waterloo, 1808–15* (Mechanicsburg, PA: Stackpole Books, 1999)

—, *Wellington's Regiments: The Men and their Battles from Roliça to Waterloo, 1805–15* (Staplehurst: Spellmount, 1994)

Forrest, Alan, *Napoleon's Men: The Soldiers of the Revolution and Empire* (New York: Hambledown, 2002)

Fremont-Barnes, Gregory (ed.) *Armies of the Napoleonic Wars* (London: Pen and Sword, 2011)

—, (ed.) T*he Encyclopedia of the French Revolutionary and Napoleonic Wars*, 3 vols (Oxford: ABC-CLIO, 2006)

—, *The French Revolutionary Wars* (Oxford: Osprey Publishing, 2001)

—, *The Napoleonic Wars: The Fall of the French Empire, 1813–1815* (Oxford: Osprey Publishing, 2002)

—, *The Napoleonic Wars: The Peninsular War, 1807–1814* (Oxford: Osprey Publishing, 2002)

Gillespie-Payne, Jonathan, *Waterloo: In the Footsteps of the Commanders* (London: Leo Cooper, 2004)

Hamilton-Williams, David, *Waterloo: New Perspectives, the Great Battle Reappraised* (London: Arms and Armour, 1993)

Haythornthwaite, Philip, *Uniforms of Waterloo* (London: Weidenfield and Nicolson, 1996)

—, *The Waterloo Armies: Men, Organisation and Tactics* (South Yorkshire: Pen & Sword, 2007)

—, *Waterloo Men: The Experience of Battle, 16–18 June 1815* (Ramsbury: Crowood Press, 1999)

Herold, Christopher, *The Battle of Waterloo* (London: Cassell, 1967)

Hibbert, Christopher, *Waterloo: Napoleon's Last Campaign* (Blue Ridge Summit, PA: Cooper Square, 2004)

Hofschröer, Peter, 1815, *The Waterloo Campaign: The German Victory* (London: Greenhill, 1997)

—, *1815, The Waterloo Campaign: Wellington, His German Allies and the Battles of Ligny and Quatre Bras* (London: Greenhill, 1997)

—, *Wellington's Smallest Victory: The Duke, the Model Maker and the Secret of Waterloo* (London: Faber and Faber, 2004)

Holmes, Richard, *Wellington: The Iron Duke* (London: HarperCollins, 2003)

Houssaye, Henry, *Napoleon and the Campaign of 1815: Waterloo* (Uckfield: Naval and Military Press, 2005)

Howarth, David, *Waterloo: A Near Run Thing* (London: Weidenfeld and Nicolson, 2003)

Keegan, John, *The Face of Battle* (London: Cape, 1976)

King, David, *Vienna 1814: How the Conquerors of Napoleon made Love, War and Peace at the Congress of Vienna* (New York: Broadway Books, 2009)

# Further Reading

Kissinger, Henry, *A World Restored: Metternich, Castlereagh and the Problems of Peace, 1812–22* (London: Weidenfeld & Nicolson, 2000)

Lachouque, Henry, *Waterloo* (London: Arms and Armour Press, 1978)

Longford, Elizabeth, *Wellington: The Years of the Sword* (London: Weidenfeld and Nicolson, 1973)

Naylor, John, *Waterloo* (London: Batsford, 1960)

Neillands, Robin, *Wellington and Napoleon: Clash of Arms, 1807–1815* (London: John Murray, 1994)

Nicolson, Harold, *The Congress of Vienna: A Study in Allied Unity, 1812–1822* (London: Faber & Faber, 2009)

Nofi, Albert, *The Waterloo Campaign: June 1815* (New York: Da Capo Press, 1998)

Nosworthy, Brent, *Battle Tactics of Napoleon and His Enemies* (London: Constable, 1998)

Paget, Julian, *Hougoumont* (London: Leo Cooper, 1992)

Pericolli, Ugo, *1815: The Armies at Waterloo* (London: Seeley Service, 1973)

Roberts, Andrew, *Napoleon and Wellington: The Long Duel* (London: Weidenfeld and Nicolson, 2003)

—, *Waterloo: Napoleon's Last Gamble* (London: HarperCollins, 2005)

Robinson, Mike, *The Battle of Quatre Bras 1815* (Stroud: The History Press, 2010)

Schom, Alan, *One Hundred Days: Napoleon's Road to Waterloo* (Oxford: Oxford University Press, 1993)

Siborne, William, *History of the Waterloo Campaign* (London: Greenhill, [1891] 1990)

Smith, Digby, *Charge! Great Cavalry Charges of the Napoleonic Wars* (London: Greenhill, 2003)

Summerville, Christopher, *Who was Who at Waterloo: A Biography of the Battle* (Essex: Longman, 2007)

Uffindell, Andrew, *The Eagle's Last Triumph: Napoleon's Victory at Ligny, June 1815* (London: Greenhill, 1994)

Uffindell, Andrew, and Michael Corum, *On the Fields of Glory: The Battlefields of the Waterloo Campaign* (London: Greenhill Books, 1996)

—, *Waterloo: The Battlefield Guide* (South Yorkshire: Pen & Sword, 2003)

Ward, S.G., *Wellington's Headquarters* (Oxford: Oxford University Press, 1957)

Weller, Jac, *Wellington at Waterloo* (London: Greenhill Books, 1992)

—, *On Wellington: The Duke and his Art of War* (London: Greenhill Books, 1998)

Wooten, Geoffrey, *Waterloo 1815* (Oxford: Osprey Publishing, 1992)

Young, Peter, *Blücher's Army, 1813–15* (London: Osprey Publishing, 1972)

Zamoyski, Adam, *Rites of Peace: The Fall of Napoleon and the Congress of Vienna* (London: Harper Perennial, 2008)

# INDEX

# Index